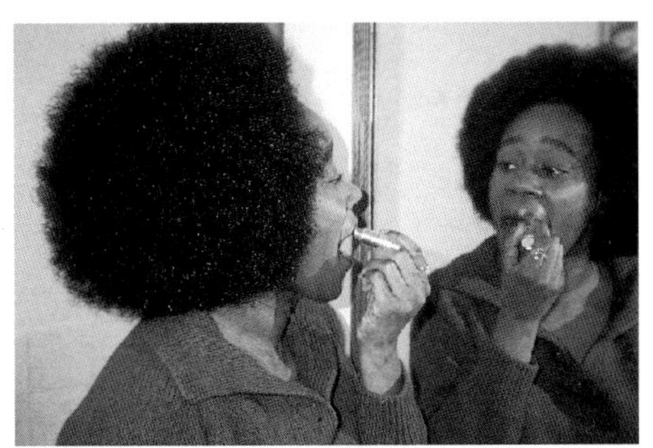

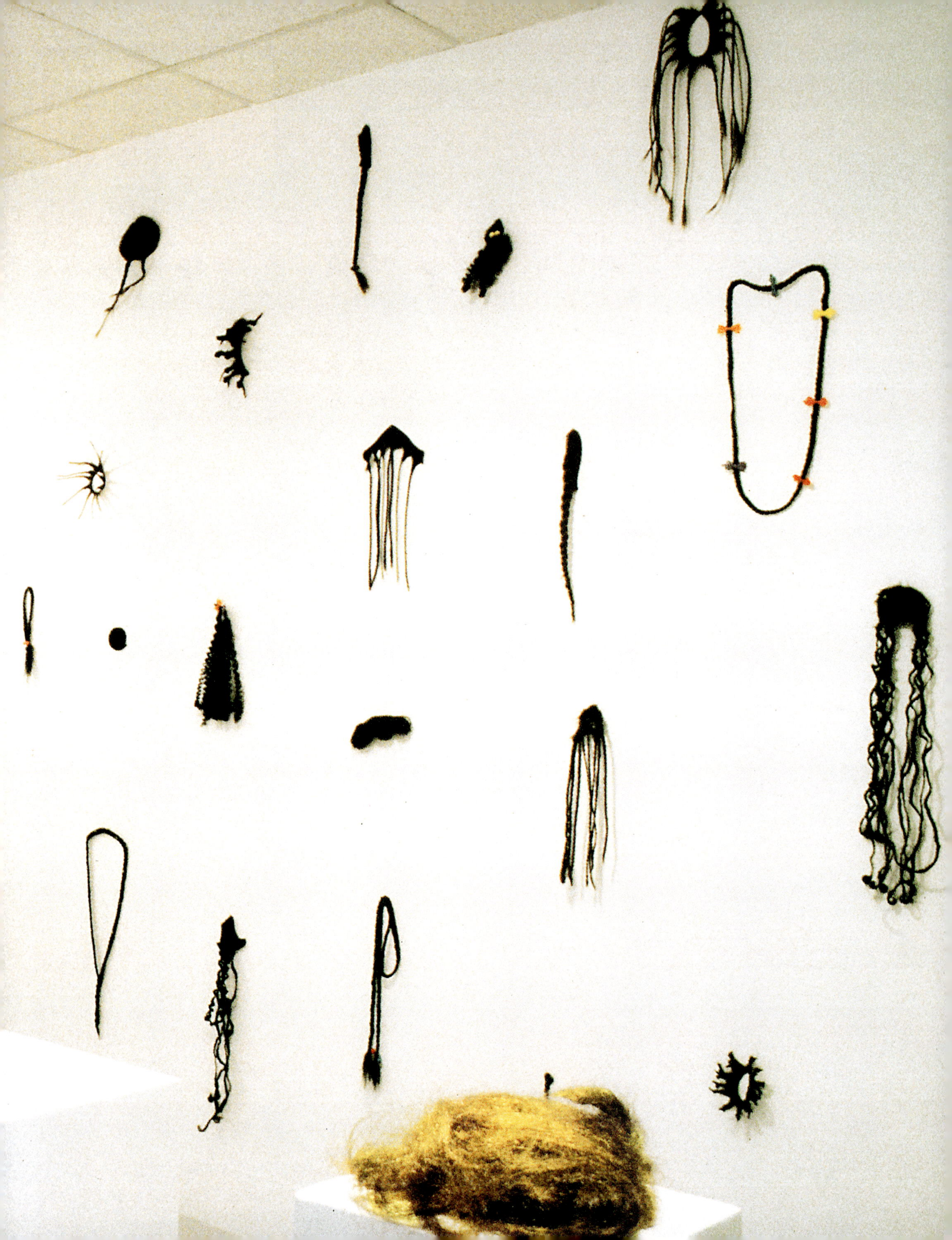

Sonia Boyce

Speaking in Tongues

Gilane Tawadros

Kala Press

For Vicky Tawadros

First published in 1997 by
KALA PRESS, PO BOX 3509, LONDON NW6 3PQ

© 1997 Sonia Boyce, Gilane Tawadros and Kala Press

ISBN 0-947753-09-5

British Library Cataloguing in Publication Data
A catalogue record for this book is available
from the British Library.

This book is published under
the Arts Council of England's
Publishing Franchise for INIVA.

Designed by Herman Lelie
Typeset by Stefania Bonelli
Production coordinated by Uwe Kraus GmbH
Printed in Italy

Front cover: *Plaited Hair* (detail) 1995
Back cover: *Three Legs Of Tights Stuffed With Hair* 1995

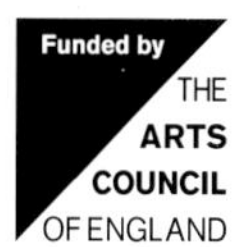

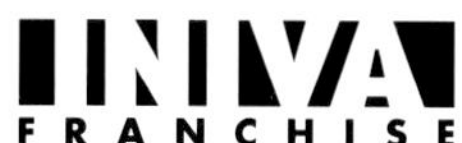

Contents

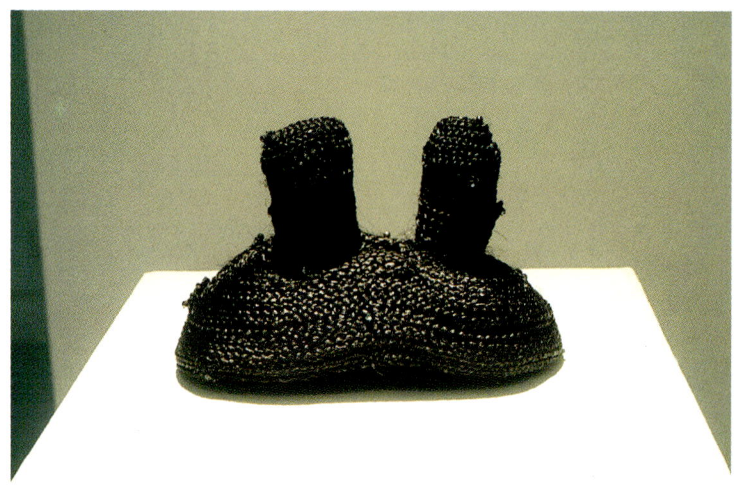

The Comforter 1993
hair, beads and velvet

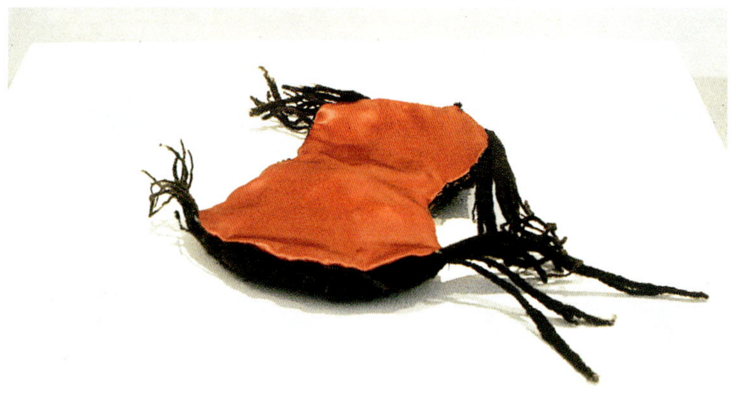

**Plaited And Sewn With
Red Satin Belly** 1993
hair and satin

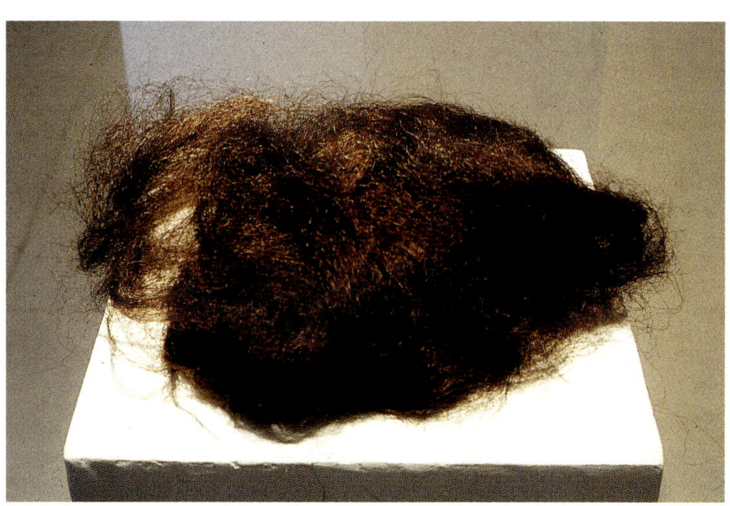

Mop Of Hair 1993
hair

Objects of Desire

> The loner who both observes and creates worlds necessarily
> speaks with many tongues. It is with these tongues that she
> explores the contours of the centres and the margins, the
> signs for somewhere and elsewhere and here and now.
>
> Deborah Levy, from 'Riding the Tiger' in *Swallowing Geography*

Some hang like pictures on the wall; others are mounted on pedestals like antique sculptures. This should not be altogether surprising. This is, after all, an art gallery. But these are not paintings or sculptures in any conventional sense. Entering the gallery from the street, you could be forgiven for mistaking Sonia Boyce's exhibition *do you want to touch?* for the obscure corner of an anthropological museum or perhaps the dusty display of an old hairdresser's shop window.[1] Boyce's works are unsettling, unnamed and indefinable objects made of hair. No two are the same: a blonde hair piece, shaped like a rib cage, bursts into a cascade of yellow wisps; another, moulded from dark brown braided hair and decorated with multi-coloured gemstones, sits on its pedestal defying all categorisation. They have the air of magical objects which transform themselves in your imagination. In the alchemy of my mind's eye, another blonde hair piece becomes a multi-tentacled octopus crawling along the seabed; yet another lined with lurid pink satin is a female warrior's armour-plate of woven hair. The exhibition invites the viewer to touch the works which, unusually for a gallery or museum space, sit unguarded by glass cases or ropes or signs warning visitors not to touch. They invite the viewer's personal fantasies and imaginings and, above all, the desire to touch. As such, they are the ultimate fetish objects.

Boyce began to make the hair pieces in 1990 without any preconceived idea of their function or significance, or how they related to her earlier body of work. Rather they evolved out of her 'doodling with hair'.[2] Boyce describes her own desire, as an artist, to touch and be in touch with materials in a more physical way than earlier works which employ photographic processes or video where 'the process itself was like taking my hand away in some way'.[3] In this respect, the hair pieces recall Boyce's early pastel drawings which

A number of major things happened while I was in my final year at art college. The First National Black Art Convention organised by the BLK Art Group Eddie Chambers Claudette Johnson Keith Piper Donald Rodney Marlene Smith (1982)

I also met Lubaina Himid and Claire Joseph (who was at college with Eddie George and Trevor Mathison) at the Black Art Convention. (1982)

relied almost entirely upon the artist's hand for their existence and which played upon an ambivalent notion of feminine arts and crafts.[4] They develop some other familiar themes in Boyce's work: the relationship between private and public; the 'spectacular' triangle between artist, viewer and object; the tension between what is familiar and comfortable on the one hand; and on the other, the unease and discomfort of what is unknown or unrecognisable. Objects of desire and objects of fear at one and the same time, the hair pieces balance precariously on the edge of humour and terror, the playful wigs and unconventional toys metamorphosing into human scalps and fragments of absent bodies.

Yet the most visible absence is the artist herself. A continuous presence in the pastel drawings of the 1980s, Boyce is not physically present in these later works except as a trace, a fragment of herself. As the artist explains, this is part of a self-conscious withdrawal of her person from the frame of her work: 'I'm not abandoning photographic processes… but I think I needed to get away from it being so intimately personal, or appearing to be so intimately personal. I don't want people to be able to point at me physically and say that's you there… they might know who I am but not because my face is in the work.'[5] The physical absence of the artist's face and body (or, indeed, of a realist depiction of an individual) from her work seems to be a radical departure from works like *Big Women's Talk* (1984), *Missionary Position I & II* (1985) and *She Ain't Holding Them Up – She's Holding On (Some English Rose)* (1986) where Boyce pictures herself literally in the central frame of these images.

Enclosed in an intimate but claustrophobic domestic space surrounded by members of her family, Boyce gazes directly at the viewer out of the frame of *She Ain't Holding Them Up* but her role both as artist and as protagonist in the picture's narrative is ambiguous. Although this work and others of the same period were interpreted as unequivocally positive and celebratory images of black family life by Boyce's contemporaries, it is far from clear whether the artist is literally holding up this image of domestic unity or holding on to an idealised memory and invented past which she has re-staged in her imagination. The family is suspended in Boyce's pictorial space which breaks up and curls away from the frame at its edges like a stage curtain revealing at its furthest corners (clasped in the beaks of two yellow birds) the barest hint of a tropical island. Caught between past

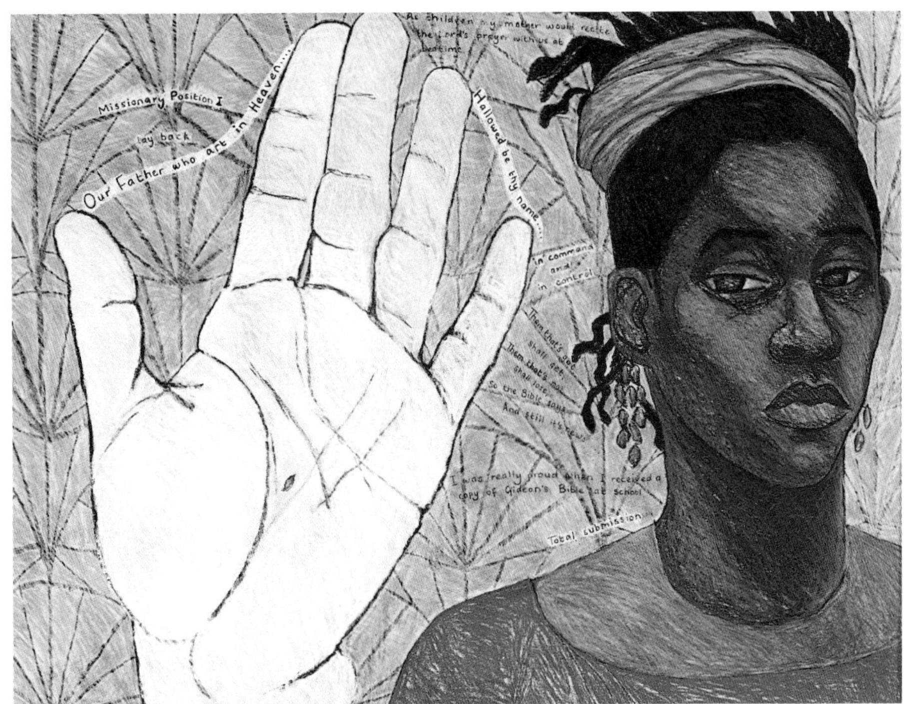

Missionary Position I – Lay Back 1985
pastels on paper

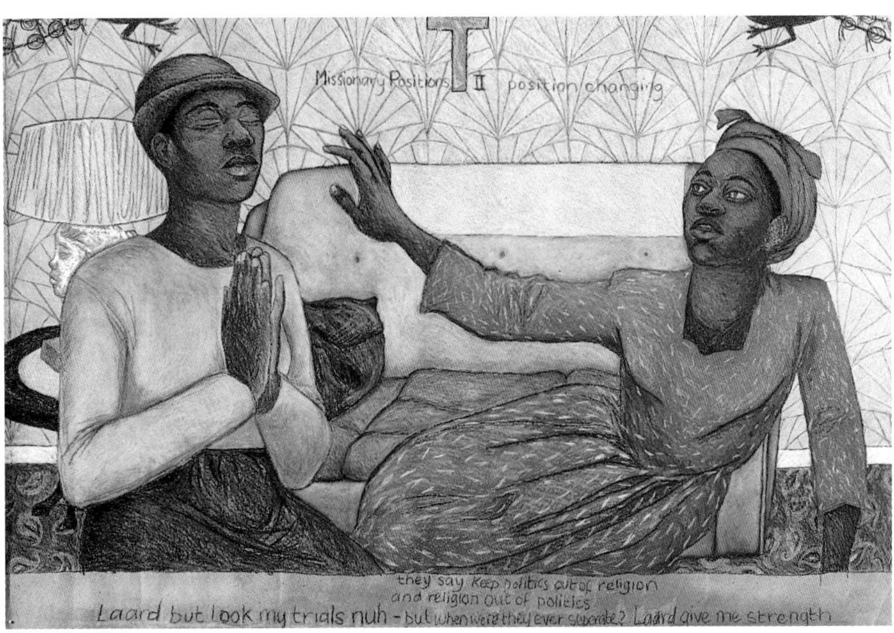

Missionary Position II – Position Changing 1985
pastels on paper

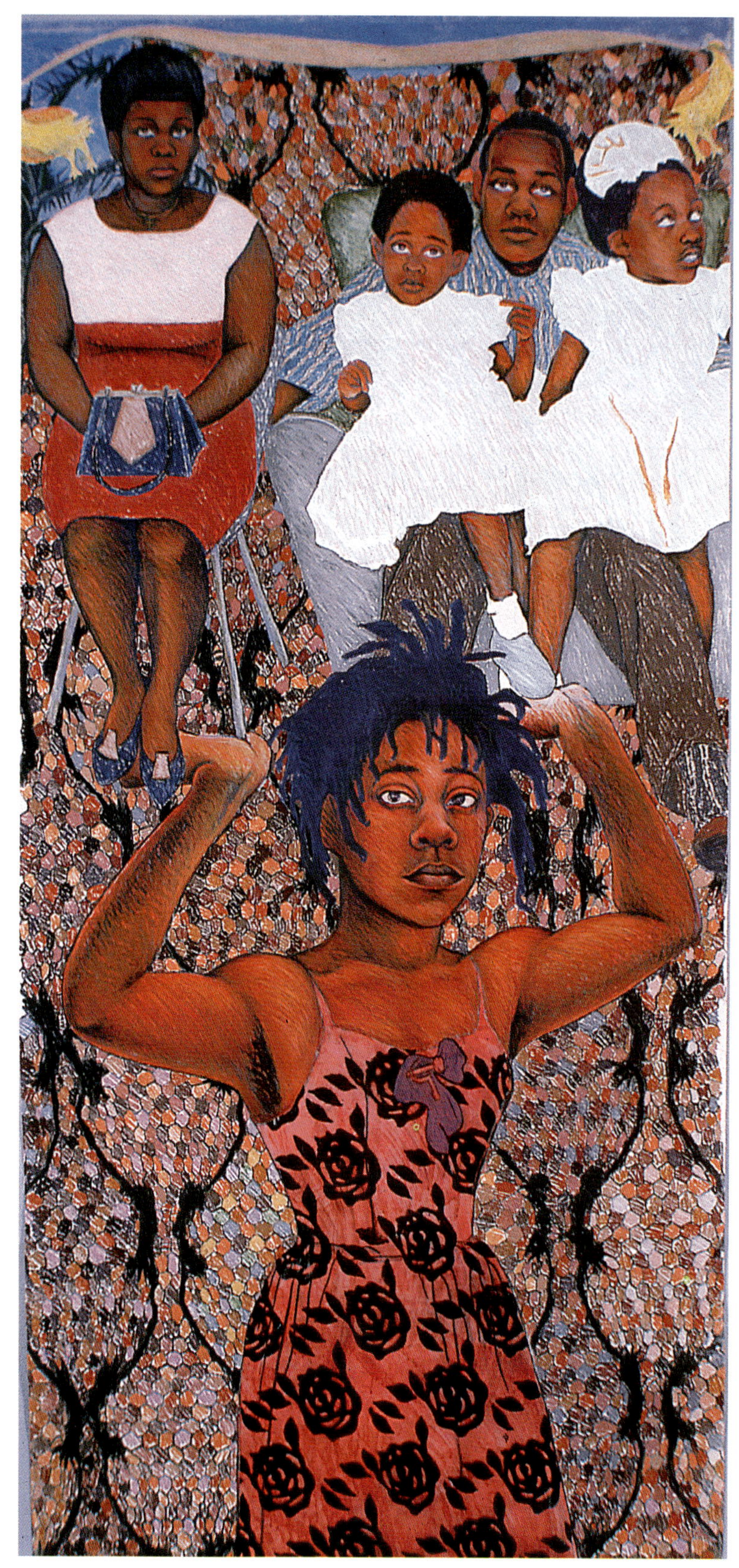

**She Ain't Holding Them Up,
She's Holding On
(Some English Rose)** 1986
pastels on paper

and present, between England and the Caribbean, this work demarcates an in-between space where competing narratives collide, become entangled but are not necessarily resolved.[6]

Attracted by the Surrealists' play on the contingent but contradictory relationship between appearance and reality and the possibilities offered by their manipulation of the real world to create a disjuncture through words and images, Boyce's early works reveal the influence of the painter René Magritte. *She Ain't Holding Them Up* echoes Magritte's *La trahison des images (The treachery of images)* of 1935. Re-interpreting the Belgian artist's proposition that 'there is very little connection between an object and what it represents',[7] Boyce here explores the relationship between an idealised notion of the family and our real experience of it, between the apparent linguistic neutrality of 'Englishness' and its actual contradictions. For Boyce, the dividing line between appearance and reality, between a private and a public space is a false one. *She Ain't Holding Them Up* explores the idea of 'home' as a domestic space but equally as a public space – both real and imagined – to which black people in the British Empire came home in significant numbers in the post-war years. As the artist writes, 'the world itself enters my home. My family, compact and complex, acts, reacts, reflects. I, in turn, interpret the world outwardly in lines, tone and colour.'[8]

For Boyce, as for other black women artists of her generation, the paintings of the Mexican artist Frida Kahlo and in particular the self-portraits she made in the 1930s, have played an important part in her artistic development. In recent years, Kahlo has become the high priestess of feminist art history, presiding over the re-writing of the art historical canon and the imperative of women artists to represent themselves. Yet, this reverence for Kahlo as well as the proliferation of self-portraits by contemporary women artists in the late 1980s and early 1990s, obscures the differing attitudes to representation which preoccupied women artists in the early 1980s. Frida Kahlo is critically absent from Rozsika Parker and Griselda Pollock's highly influential book *Old Mistresses: Women, Art and Ideology*, first published in 1981, which articulated the increasing unease of a significant number of white feminist artists and art historians with the depiction of the female body and particularly the female nude:

In art the female nude parallels the effects of the feminine stereotype in art historical discourse. Both confirm male dominance. As female nude, woman is body, is nature opposed to male culture, which in turn is represented by the very act of transforming nature, that is, the female model or motif, into the ordered forms and colour of a cultural artefact, a work of art.[9]

Artists like Mary Kelly whose work is cited by Parker and Pollock as 'an example of a feminist artist who has taken up the issues of radical practice in art', opposed the idea of women using or making images of women's bodies and in her widely cited project *Post Partum Document* of 1976, Kelly purposely eschewed conventional pictorial representation, employing instead diagrams, graphs and texts to map the first six years of her son's life.

The attitude of black women artists to the issue of self-representation in the early Eighties was more closely aligned to that of artists like Cindy Sherman whose untitled black and white studies for film stills of the late '70s picture the artist as the heroine of '40s and '50s Hollywood 'B' movies, or series of colour 'centrefolds' of the early Eighties pointed to the unstable and shifting quality of identity and the ambivalence of the female artist's dual role as both image and image-maker, object and subject.

Representing oneself and representing the black female body was a central and urgent issue for the artist Lubaina Himid whom Boyce met for the first time at the First National Black Art Convention which took place at Wolverhampton Polytechnic in October 1982. The conference marked a turning point in Boyce's development as an artist. She was in the third year of a Fine Art degree course at Stourbridge College of Art and Technology where she had no access to information about contemporary black artists, had little contact with other black art students and consequently felt very isolated:

> Both on foundation and at Stourbridge I spent a lot of time in the library trying to track down some information on contemporary black visual artists. However, although I found books on traditional African and Indian art, and so-called 'primitive' art, and two books on Afro-American art, which has a long history dating back to the 1700s, there was nothing on contemporary black art in Britain. The sense of relief and

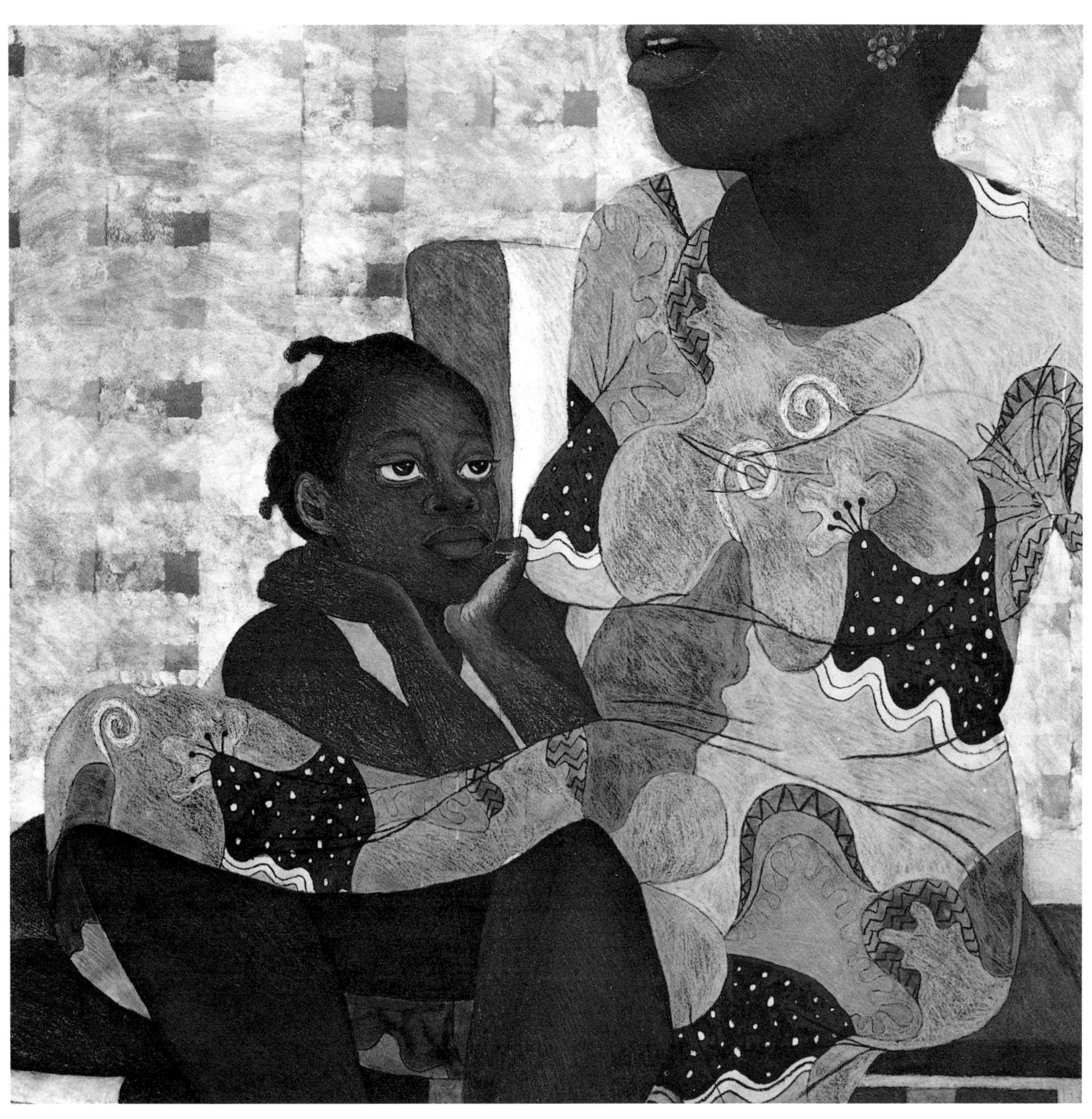

Big Women's Talk 1984
pastels on paper

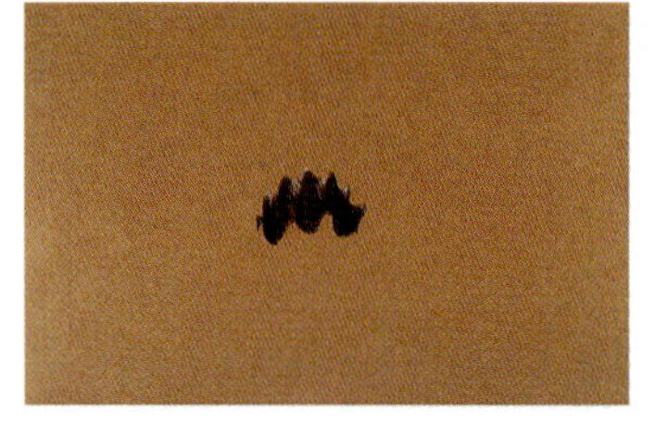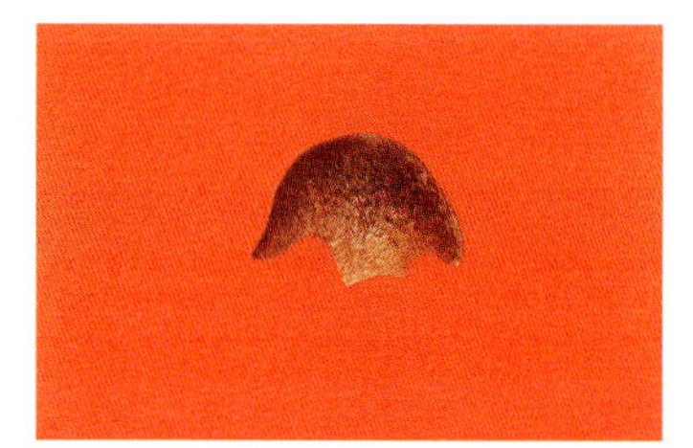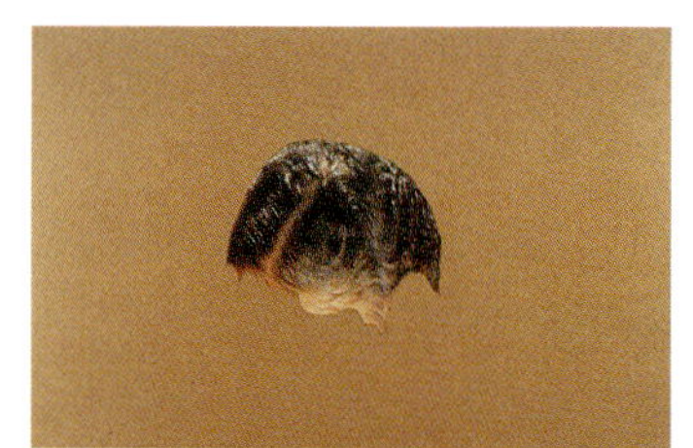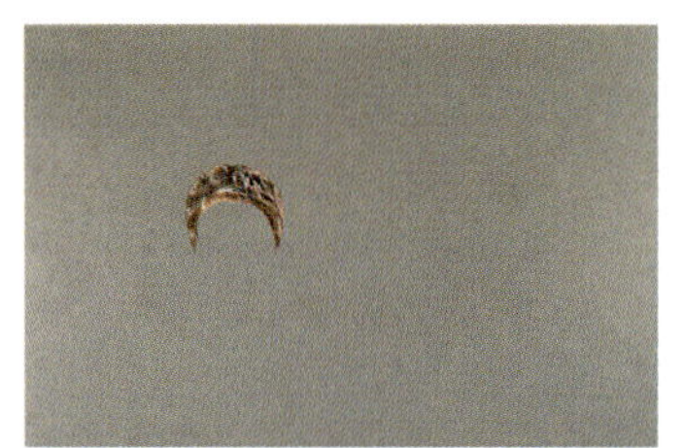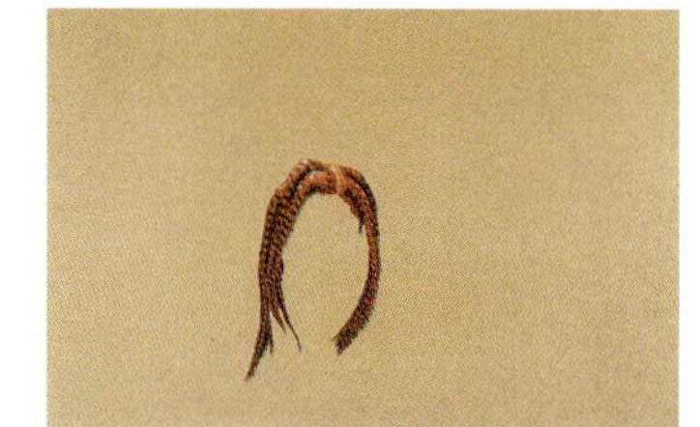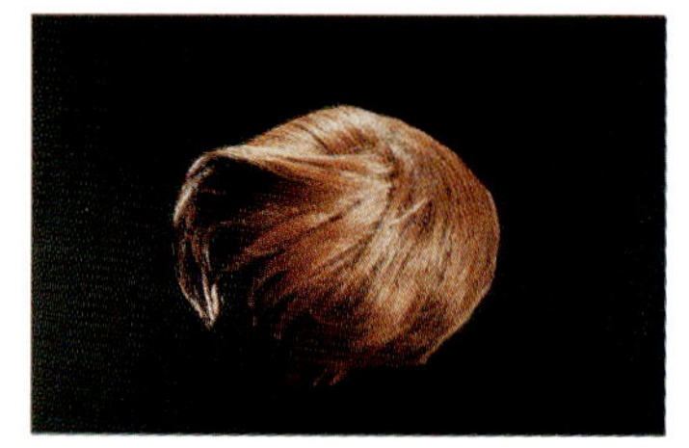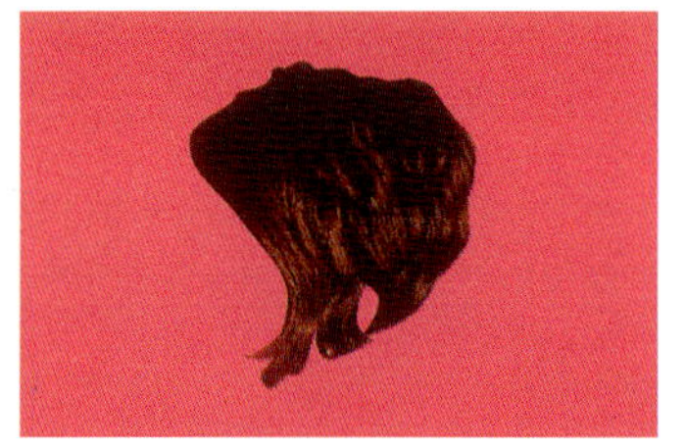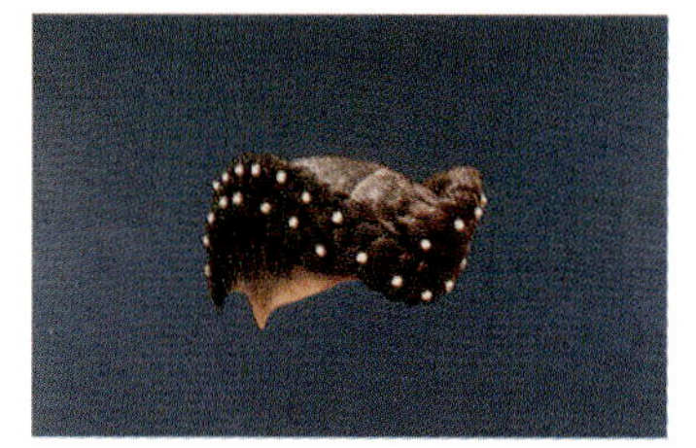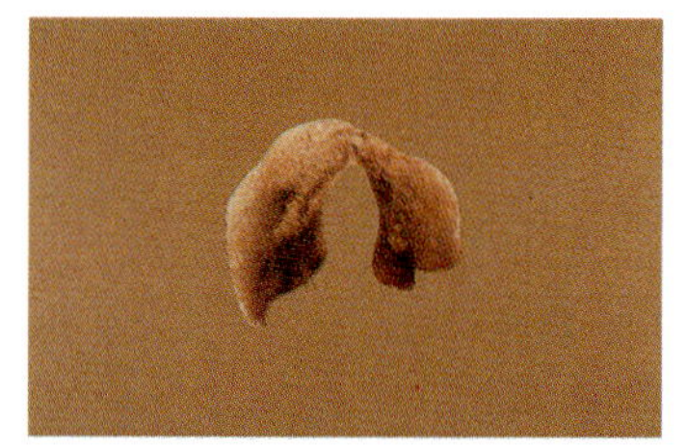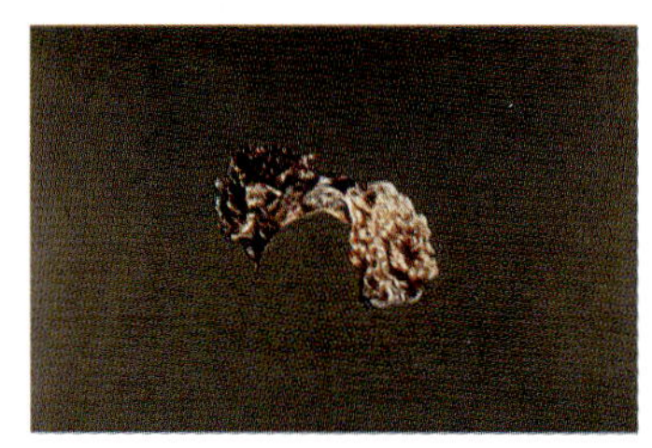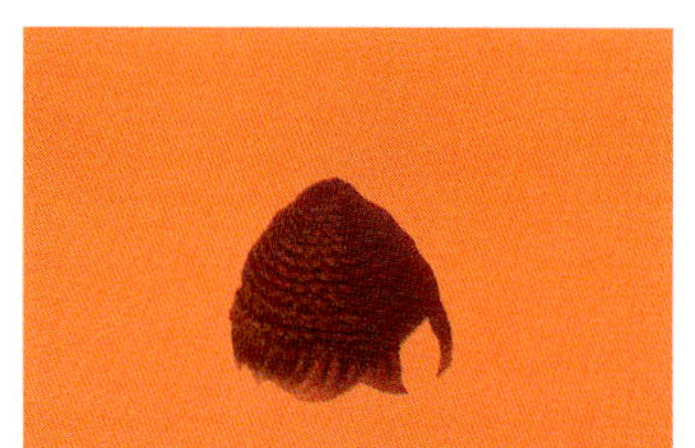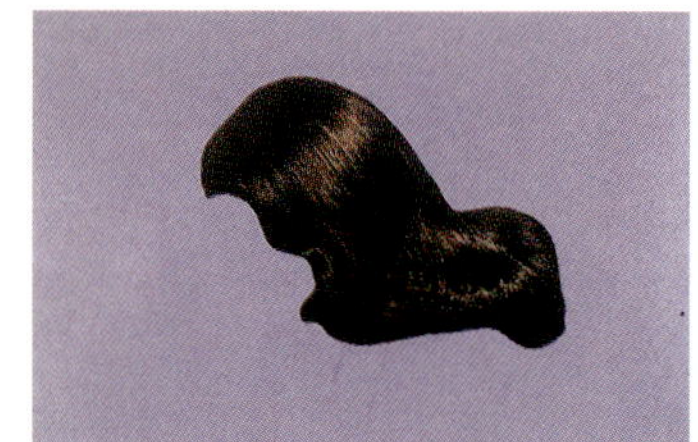

Black Female Hairstyles 1995
collages

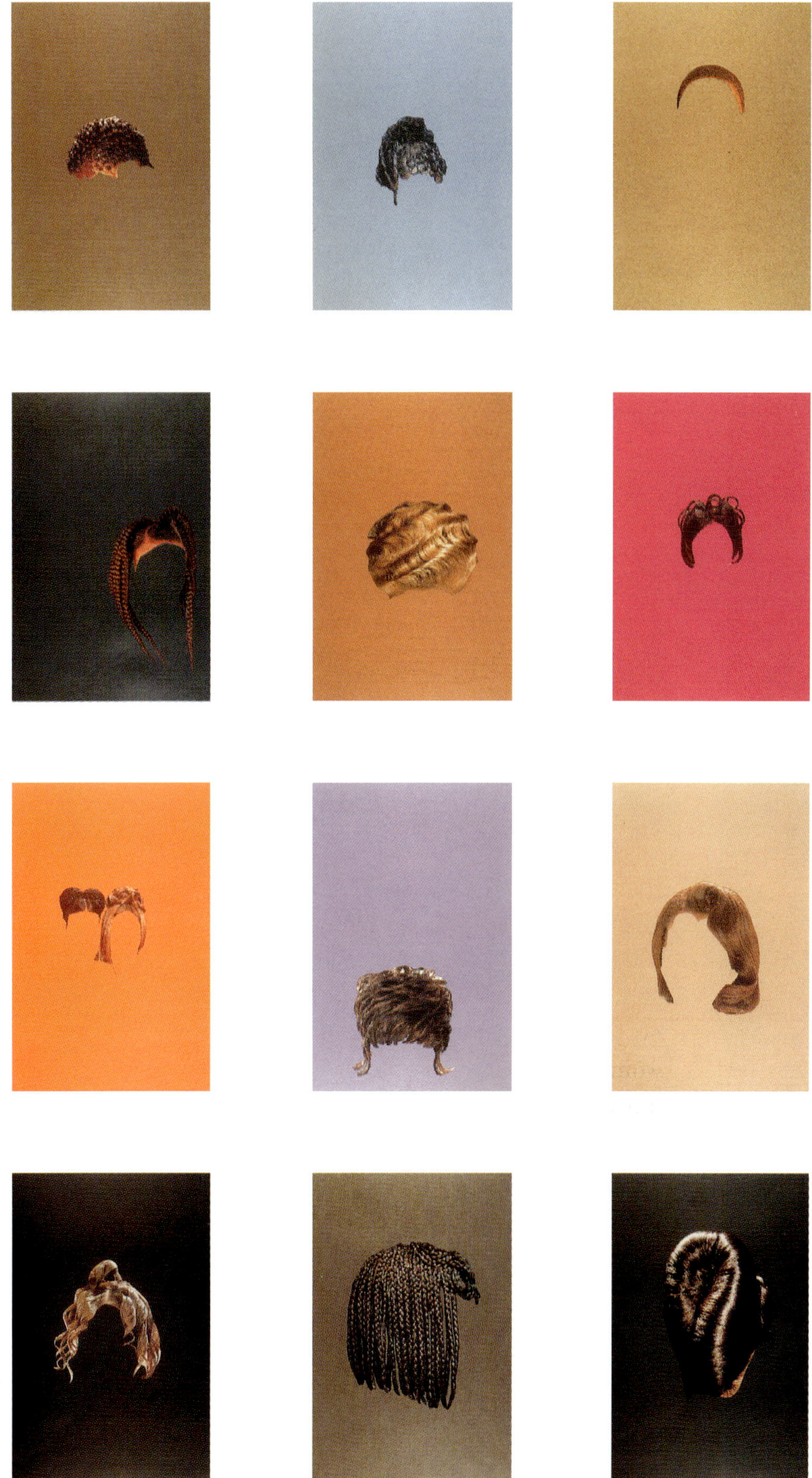

exhilaration when I walked into that first conference; seeing so many black artists there! It's very easy to orientate yourself towards the Eurocentric distortions of art history at college particularly when there is no visible alternative. Consequently, it was difficult for me to know where I stood. How could I start to work with the ideas I had? How was I to start? The Pan African Connection [sic] offered a glimpse of what was possible, but I was not able to work in that way… What often happened at college was that if you were working in a certain area, dealing with social issues, you were persuaded to work with photography regardless of whether the style or the content was sympathetic to that kind of format. Many people were sent down to the photography department and never seen again. I decided I was not going to do that.[10]

The Wolverhampton conference had been organised by the Pan-Afrikan Connection (a group of young black artists which included Eddie Chambers, Claudette Johnson, Wenda Lesley, Marlene Smith and Keith Piper) to discuss the form, function and future of black art in Britain. The conference came as a revelation to Boyce who subsequently showed her work publicly for the first time the following year in a women's group exhibition at the Africa Centre, organised and selected by Lubaina Himid.[11] During the mid-Eighties, Boyce developed her own artistic idiom in the context of an emerging and increasingly visible black arts movement. In the work of many black artists at this time (both men and women), the black body takes centre stage.[12] While a number of white feminist artists, although by no means all, had rejected the depiction of the female body, black women artists defiantly insisted on the centrality of black women in the very frame of representation. Long before 'bad girls' emerged on the 1990s art scene in London and New York contesting the hard edged and didactic art of their '80s feminist precursors like Barbara Kruger and Jenny Holzer, artists like Sonia Boyce, Sutapa Biswas, Lubaina Himid and Claudette Johnson to name a few, were articulating an assertive black female sexuality in their work.[13] Essentially 'feminine' materials such as fabric, pastels, chalks and decorative paper were mobilised by these artists to create works which were monumental both in their physical scale and in their political scope. Like patchwork and collage, the use of pastels

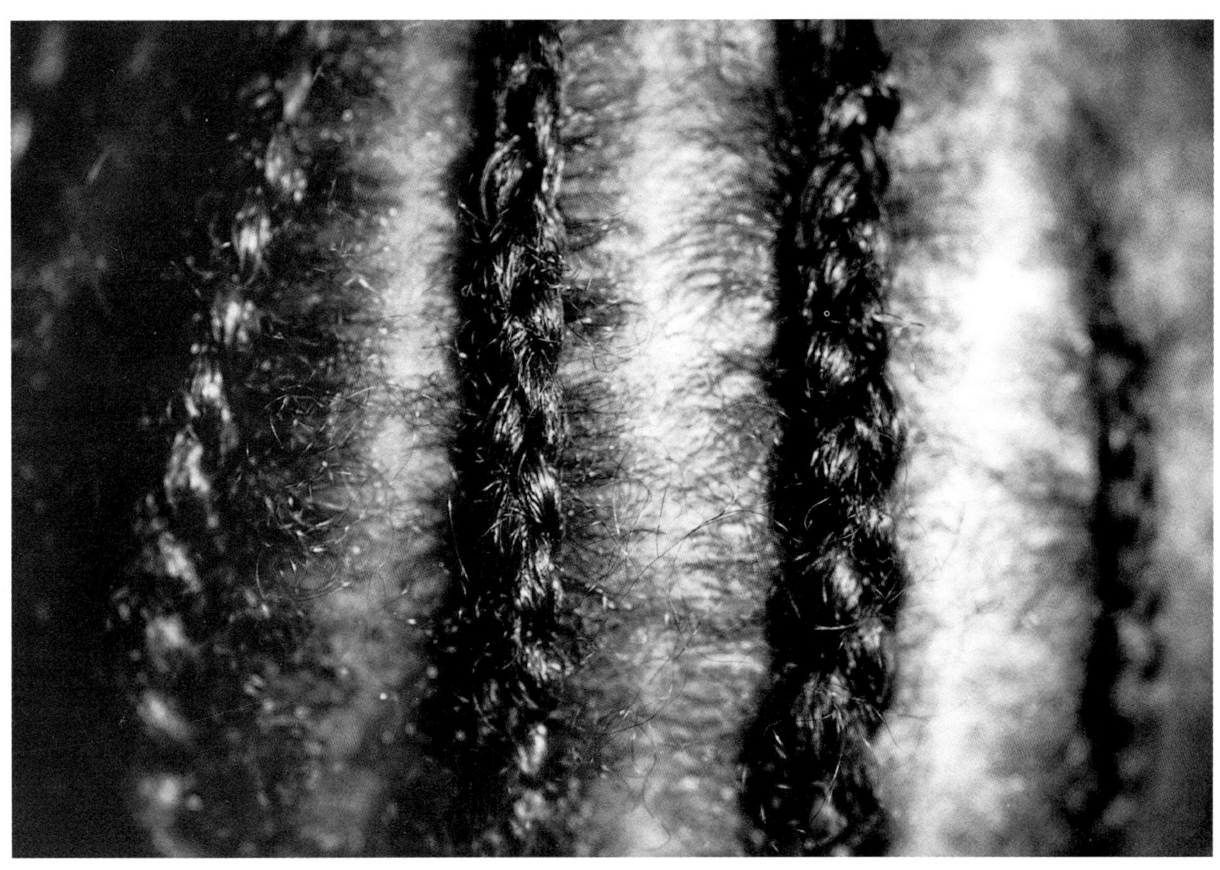

Plaited Hair 1995
Black and white
photograph

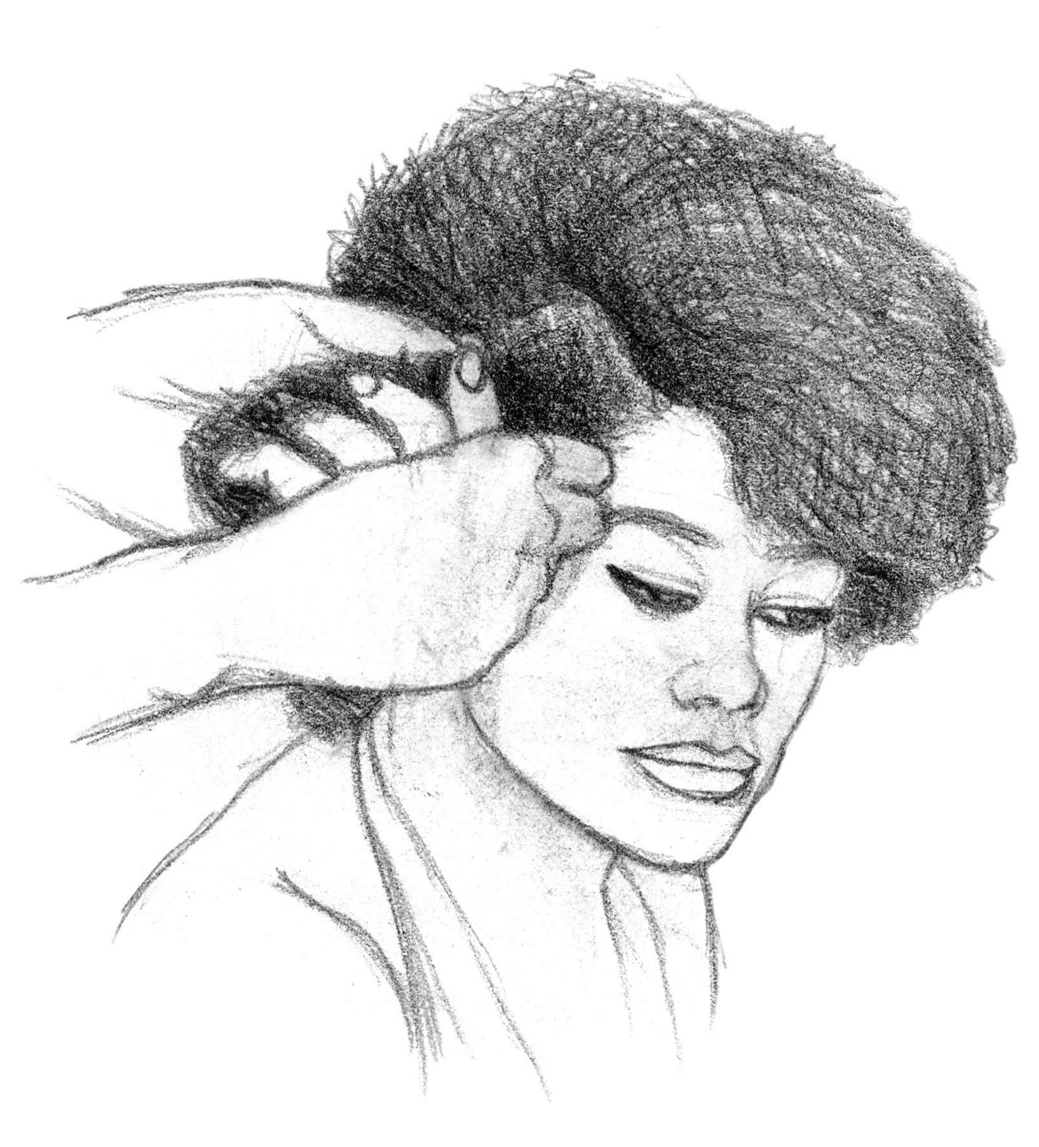

drawing from sketchbook
1986

reinforced the idea of an ambivalent femininity which defied simplistic categorisation as inherently passive and apolitical. In this context, the home and domestic environment could be seen as a space in which the past and present become fused together. The domestic realm is perceived as a manifestly political space where there is no comfort from the configurations of history or lived experience. And at the point where the domestic is seen to be political, the 'feminine' becomes politically resistant. Thus, the woman in Boyce's *In the Comfort of Your Own Home* (1986) metamorphoses into a Medusa-like figure with a serpent's tongue, or more appropriately, a Medea-like figure – the woman of Greek mythology who is marginalised from the hegemonic order of Corinthian society on the basis of her avowed cultural difference. The woman whose resistance, furthermore, takes the form of a transfiguration of perceived notions of 'femininity' and 'domesticity'.[14]

With her recent hair sculptures, Boyce returns us to the realm of Greek mythology and to a post-Freudian world where fantasy cannot be easily extrapolated from reality and where the part does not necessarily stand in for the whole. They play sardonically on the difference between the sexual fetish of Freudian theory and the fetish of colonial discourse as described by Frantz Fanon in *Black Skin, White Masks*. As Homi Bhabha explains, 'the fetish of colonial discourse – what Fanon calls the epidermal schema – is not, like the sexual fetish, a secret. Skin, as the key signifier of cultural and racial difference in the stereotype, is the most visible of fetishes, recognised as common knowledge in a range of cultural, political, historical discourses, and plays a part in the racial drama that is enacted every day in colonial societies'.[15] Both public and private, hair occupies what Gilles Deleuze has, in another context, called a 'zone of indiscernibility' in which the seen and unseen, the sexual and racial come together in the post-colonial metropolis (a terrain to which the artist returns repeatedly).

Yet, while Boyce's hair pieces can be seen as metonymic signifiers of race, partial indicators of 'blackness' which mark the simultaneous presence and absence of black people within our society, they also defy the reduction of racial difference into a singular, undifferentiated sign. Rather, they present us with a galaxy of signs and possible readings which remain partial and inconclusive without the agency of the viewer to complete the narrative. The hair sculptures collapse the

This was also the year that I entered the realm of the black survey show. *Into The Open* was a show that opened at the Mappin Art Gallery under the directorship of Mike Tooby and with the curatorial advice of Lubaina. (1984)

distinction between the fragment and the whole, and most importantly perhaps, between the viewer and the object. The question which frames the exhibition *do you want to touch?* also frames the space which exists between the artist, the viewer and the object. The artist is absent but present, if only in part. The object could be part of the artist and the viewer – as wig or hair extension perhaps – or it could be a creature apart. It is significant that the pedestals on which some of the hair sculptures sit are quite low, accessible, within the physical reach of the viewer or potential 'toucher'. In their height, scale and accessibility, they contrast tellingly with works like those of Richard Serra, in particular his vast metal cubes which often elicit a tactile response from viewers and yet: '… are trying to avoid the body in a way, even with a male audience using their hands quite alot.'[16]

Rather than avoiding the corporeal, Boyce's work has always insisted on the primacy of the body, but whereas the body existed literally within the frame of images like *Talking Presence* (1988), the body is refigured in the artist's works of the 1990s. In some ways more literal than her early pastel drawings, the body is implicitly present as an unattributed trace of an anonymous and absent body, perhaps of the artist herself, perhaps of the viewer. In many ways, these later works recall the 'relational objects' of Lygia Clark and the Brazilian artist's own investigations of the relationship between artist and viewer which Guy Brett has described:

> The evolution of Clark's work may perhaps be summed up as a radical journey beyond the traditional relationship between artist and spectator. Traditionally, the artist is a giver of a communication and the spectator the receiver. This transaction is mediated by the 'art work'… Suppose, instead, that the artist's production was not her own encoded expressivity directed toward the other person as spectator, but provided some means for that other person to become conscious of his/her own expressivity, in the role of participant. The roles of 'artist', 'spectator' and mediating 'object' would all change. Since the object could no longer be a representation, it could have no meaning or structure outside the participants' manipulation of it in the here-and-now.[17]

Clapping Wallpaper 1994
photo silk screen on lining paper

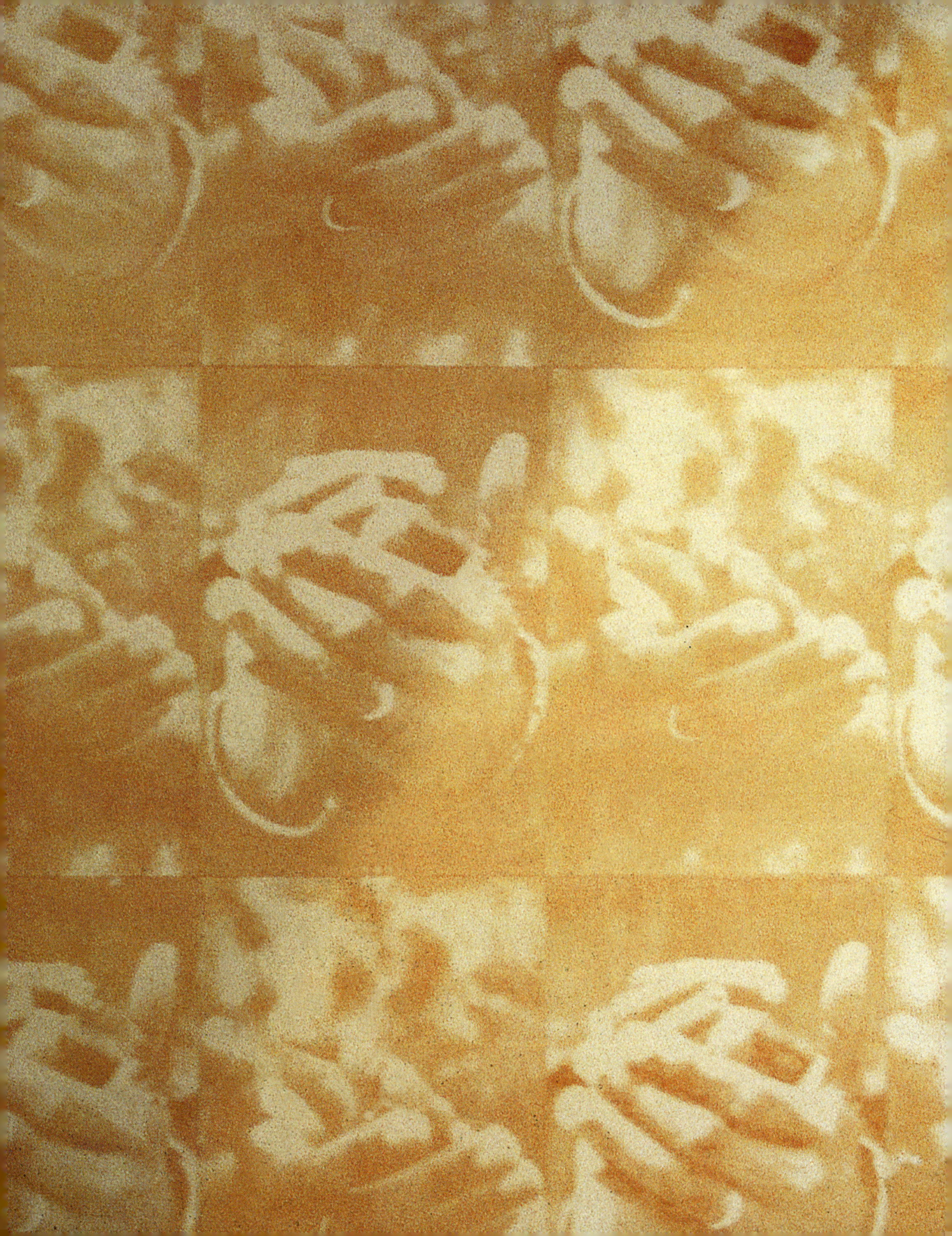

These were the heady days of GLC interventions. I was invited to be on the Visual Arts Panel of the Greater London Arts board, and was working at the Docklands Community Poster Project putting up billboards of the work of Pete Dunn and Lorraine Leeson. (1985)

In the exhibition *Wish You Were Here*, organised by the artists' group Bank in London in September 1994, Boyce took the elimination of the space between viewer and object a step further. Working collaboratively, the artists created a domestic environment in a disused warehouse space where the identity of individual artists took less prominence than the interrelationship of the works in the space. Boyce's contribution to the project consisted of a blanket of hair woven from numerous individual wigs of varying colours and styles which was strewn on a bed in one of the 'bedrooms', and the wallpaper which covered most of the communal walls in the space. Reminiscent of Boyce's earlier use of wallpaper designs, here the artist created her own wallpaper from two photographic images of clapping hands, repeated over and over again. The image of the clapping hands (dislocated from identifiable bodies) fills what is intended to be a private space. The dividing line between private and public has once again been ruptured and the audience's simultaneous absence and presence in many ways becomes the 'subject' of the work.

A few months after the Bank exhibition, Boyce staged an intervention in the Cultures Gallery of Brighton Museum and Art Gallery where the audience's agency became even more explicitly the subject of the installation. Swathing the glass cases in opaque tracing paper, Boyce temporarily obscured the ethnographic objects from view. Over a number of months, the artist traced the shadows cast by the ethnographic objects as they hung like strange fruit in the display cases so that to see the objects, the viewer was forced to move up close to the cases and peer through the uneven shapes cut out of the tracing paper. Looking through these strangely shaped openings, the view was limited, partial and incomplete and the spectator was made to feel self-conscious about the act of looking, as if the artist was determined to implicate us as peeping toms; or, perhaps, to implicate the museum itself.

Even in the late twentieth century, it seems, museums have never lost sight of their origins as cabinets of curiosities: to enter the space of the museum is to enter another world where we move from one room to the next, gazing at the exotic objects laid out before us like a sumptuous feast set out for our eyes to consume. Like delectable sweetmeats beyond our reach, these artefacts offer up the promise of unfamiliar, illicit pleasures which are visible but unattainable, to be seen but not touched. In her installation entitled *peep*, Boyce

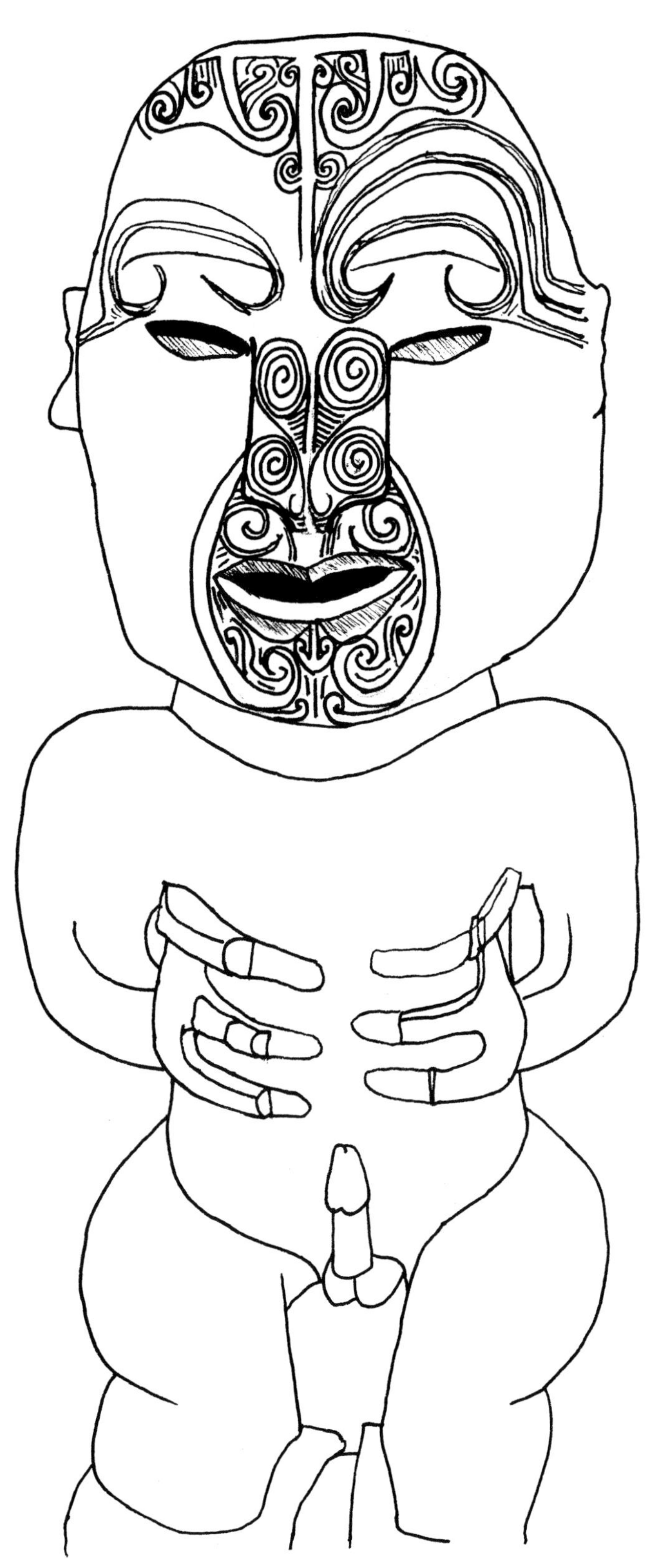

**Drawing of Ancestor
Figure** (Maori People,
New Zealand
– nineteenth century)
Brighton Museum 1995

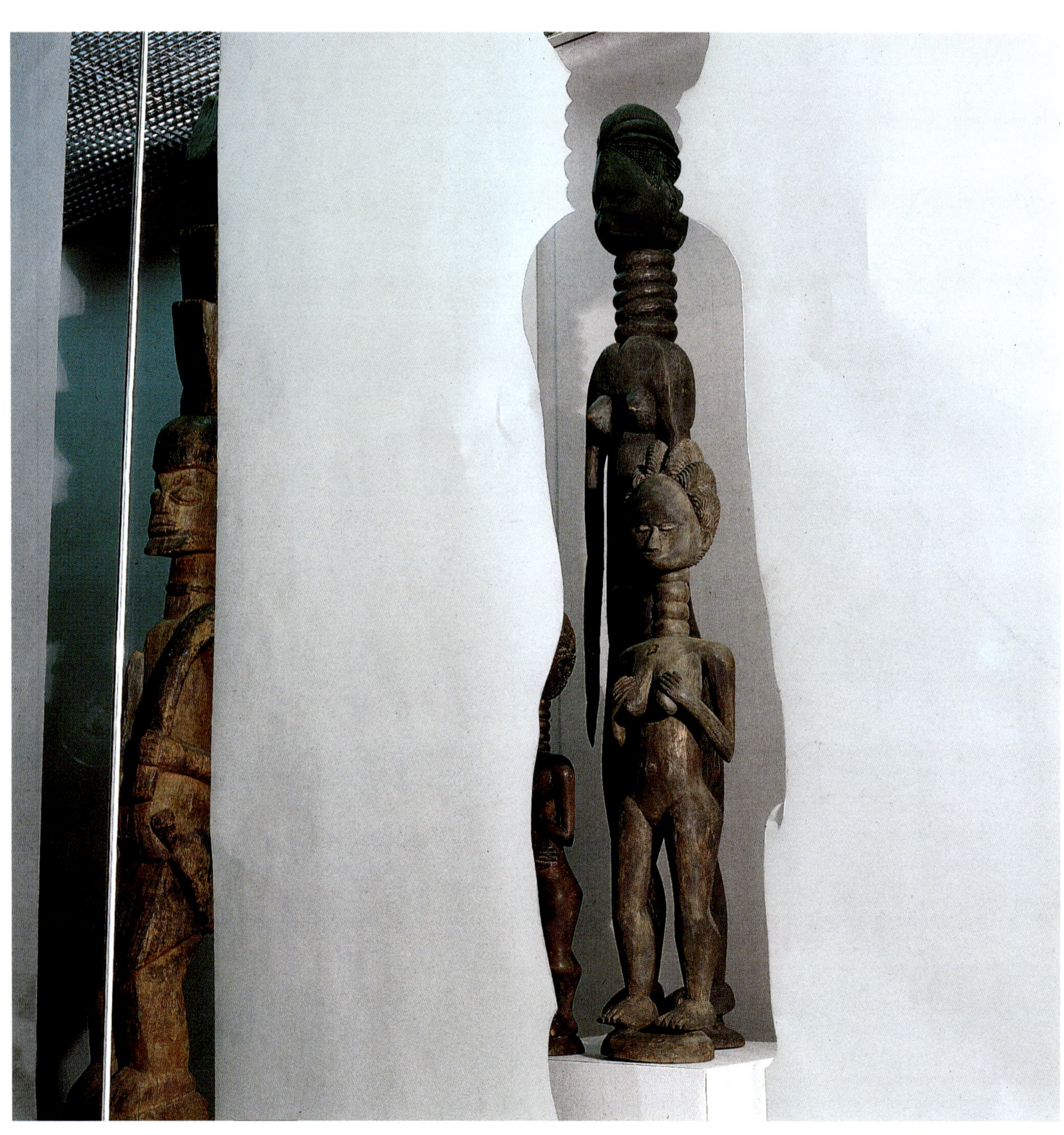

installation view of **peep**, Cultures Gallery,
Brighton Museum 1995
cut outs from tracing paper

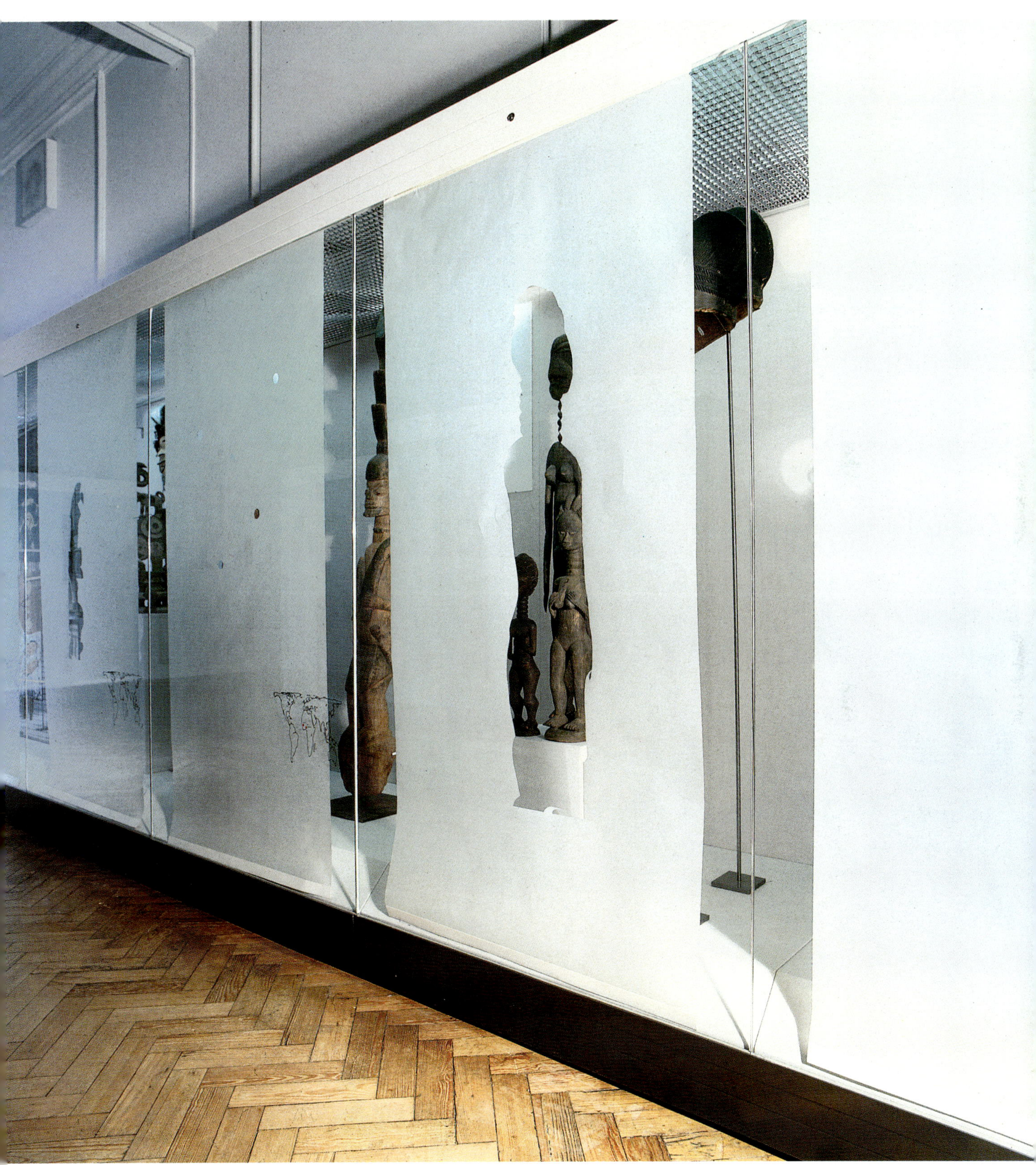

circumscribed the visitor's gaze, forcing us to acknowledge the very act of looking in a museum as an illicit act. To look in Boyce's museum space is to engage in a compelling but somewhat dubious activity. At first glance, on entering the space, one's gaze falls not on the objects or on the display cases but rather on other visitors caught in the act of looking.

It is by looking through the elongated silhouettes cut out of the tracing paper that we are able to see the museum artefacts and the artist's own works alongside. It is as if these objects, removed to the museum space and tinged with a melancholic aura, have been reduced to shadows of their former selves, like freaks at a peep show which we can never fully see or understand. Our view of these objects, it seems, is inevitably partial and obscured and our role as viewers inevitably that of compliant voyeurs:

> I wasn't paying much attention at first, they were making hushed noises in groups. Eventually I noticed that there was a large group gathered in the corner giggling. After they'd left I saw that they had been looking at the Maori Ancestor figure, a large wooden sculpture of a male figure with quite intricate carvings on its face and a rather prominent erection. Of course it's so subliminal one takes it for granted. Where else but a museum or a public gallery could one see such explicit displays of sexual objects. How long had these figures, and others like them, been on display in the museum? Since the 1920s I was later told... Generation upon generation of school children encountering such illicit pleasures from educational trips.[18]

1   Sonia Boyce, *do you want to touch?*, Centre 181 Gallery,
    London, 4–27 August 1993.

2   Interview with Sonia Boyce, 6 September 1994.

3   Ibid. above.

4   For a fuller discussion of the alternative concept of femininity
    in the work of Boyce, Biswas et al., see my essay, 'Beyond
    the Boundary: The Work of Three Black Women Artists in
    Britain', *Third Text* 8/9, Autumn/Winter 1989, p.148.

5   Interview with Sonia Boyce, 6 September 1994.

6   This collision of narratives is made explicit visually in the
    different accessories worn by the two women in the picture.
    The older woman wears a cross around her neck, while the
    younger one wears a red hammer and sickle in the bow of
    her dress.

7   René Magritte, 'Les mots et les images', quoted by
    Sarah Whitfield in *Magritte*, exhibition catalogue,
    Hayward Gallery, South Bank Centre, London, 1992.

8   From *Sonia Boyce*, exhibition catalogue, Air Gallery,
    London, 1987.

9   Rozsika Parker and Griselda Pollock, *Old Mistresses:
    Women, Art and Ideology*, Routledge & Kegan Paul,
    London, 1981.

10 Sonia Boyce from John Roberts, 'Interview with Sonia Boyce',
    Third Text, 1, Autumn 1987, p.60.

11 In addition to Sonia Boyce and Lubaina Himid, the exhibition,
    which was entitled *Five Black Women Artists* living in Britain,
    also included the work of Claudette Johnson, Houria Niati
    and Veronica Ryan. The mid-Eighties were an important
    and productive period for black women artists in Britain in
    which Lubaina Himid played a vital role both as artist and
    curator. In November of the same year, she curated *Black
    Women Time Now* this time at Battersea Arts Centre as part
    of a two-week festival of black women's art and including
    fifteen artists. Two years later, she curated *The Thin Black
    Line* at the Institute of Contemporary Arts and in April 1986
    she opened an independent gallery space The Elbow Room
    in a disused warehouse in Borough, South London, with
    the exhibition *Unrecorded Truths* which included Boyce's
    *She Ain't Holding Them Up, She's Holding On (Some English
    Rose)*.

12 I am thinking here, in particular, of Keith Piper's work.
    See, for example, *Keep Singing (Another Nigger Died Today)*,
    (1982); *(You Are Now Entering) Mau Mau Country* (1983)
    and *Go West Young Man* (1988).

13 See, for example, the exhibition *Bad Girls*, Institute
    of Contemporary Arts, London, October 1993; or, the
    exhibition of the same name which opened coincidentally
    at the New Museum, New York, in January 1994.

14 See Gilane Tawadros, op.cit., p.149.

15 Homi K. Bhabha, 'The other question: Stereotype,
    discrimination and the discourse of colonialism', *The
    Location of Culture*, Routledge, London and New York,
    1994, p.78.

16 Interview with Sonia Boyce, 6 September 1994.

17 Guy Brett, 'Lygia Clark: In Search of the Body', *Art in
    America*, July 1994, p.58.

18 Sonia Boyce from *peep* exhibition catalogue, Institute
    of International Visual Arts, London 1995.

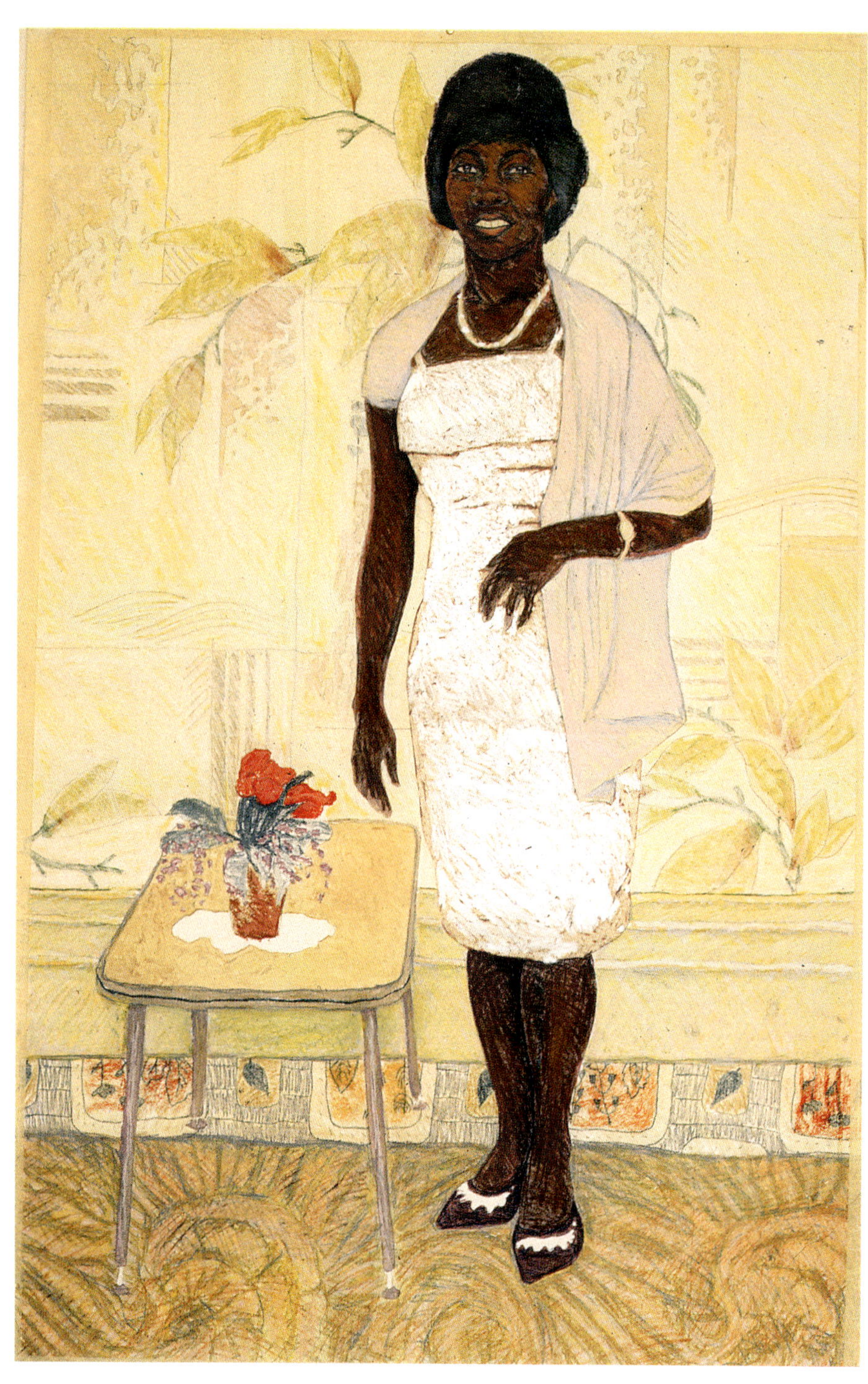

Auntie Enid – The Pose 1985
pastels on paper

Nation and Narration

Nations, like narratives, lose their origins in the myths of
time and only fully realise their horizons in the mind's eye…
the ambivalent, antagonistic perspective of nation as narration
[establishes] the cultural boundaries of the nation… as
'containing' thresholds of meaning that must be crossed,
erased, and translated in the process of cultural production…
What emerges as an effect of such 'incomplete signification'
is a turning of boundaries into the in-between spaces through
which the meanings of cultural and political authority are
negotiated… between cultures and nations, theories and
texts, the political, the poetic and the painterly, the past and
the present.[1]

Homi K. Bhabha

Steeped in sumptuous colours and intricate patterns, Boyce's figurative drawings of the mid-Eighties are rich and complex narratives which interweave the past and present, history and lived experience. Using colour, pattern and form, they present visual narratives which criss-cross space and time, transgressing the discrete borders which separate different generations, geographies and histories. *Big Women's Talk* from 1984 and *Conversational Piece: Kitchen Table Talk, Strange Dreams* from 1986 map out the intimate, domestic spaces where tales of past lives and distant places mingle in the here-and-now. But these are not complete stories, recounted from beginning to end. Rather they are snatched conversations, half-finished sentences suspended in the air; loose words, heard but not fully understood. Playing both semantically and conceptually with the traditional notion of the conversation piece, Boyce elaborates upon this eighteenth century painting genre to produce a pastel drawing which defies completeness in every way: it is a preparatory drawing for a final painting which is never to be painted; it is a domestic portrait which masks from view the identities of its protagonists; it represents a fragment in space and time which eludes any definite conclusion or, indeed, resolution.[2]

Another domestic portrait, *Big Women's Talk* pictures the artist as a young girl, resting her elbows on her mother's lap, silhouetted

**A very rocky year.
My first solo shows,
Conversations at the
Black Art Gallery and
Sonia Boyce at the
Air Gallery. I wonder
what has happened to
Shaka Deddi the former
director of the Black Art
Gallery. Iwona Blazwick
initiated the Air Gallery
show, but then moved
on to work at the ICA.
Sara Selwood then took
over, I wonder what has
happened to her now.
(1986)**

against the patterns of her dress and attentive to every word which comes out of her mother's mouth. The mother's face is beyond our view and our eyes are drawn irresistibly to her mouth at the edge of the picture frame. An invisible diagonal seems to cut across the picture plane, connecting the listening child and the speaking mother but at the same time creating a discrete space between them, circumscribing their sameness and their difference, the things they share in common and the things which set them apart. The diagonal indicates both continuity and rupture between different generations and different locations. It is a migration line, marking the point where the thread of continuous narratives has been broken by the act of migration but where, simultaneously, new narrative strands and remembered histories begin to be formed:

> I was thinking about when I was a child and how my mother used to take us to all her friends and the houses used to be really full, and kids running up and down the house, and people in the kitchen baking bread and someone else in the living room talking about back home and stuff like that. And I was thinking about how I was always sort of tagging on to my mum's skirt and listening to all these conversations, getting all the juicy bits of who did what, when. What I felt was a sort of safe time for me, like being hidden but being very secure. So I started thinking about conversations my mother used to have… this was just like a second of it, rather than encapsulating a whole story. That whole time, that whole culture that you don't see anywhere else… I'm talking about the stories and the tales that our parents brought with them when they came from the Caribbean, that whole lifestyle; it's like cutting short a continuity. They left everything and they came here, and what that means for us here. I'm from here but from there as well…[3]

Works like *Auntie Enid – the Pose* (1984) and *Cricket Days? Domino Nights!* (1986) intervene in recollections of migration and arrival and our readings of the photographic 'evidence' which all too often stand in for 'real experience'. It is precisely because these works are not photographs but rather pastel drawing and photocopy with pastel respectively that they contest the very notion of the 'real'. They are realist works approximating to the real, to the outward

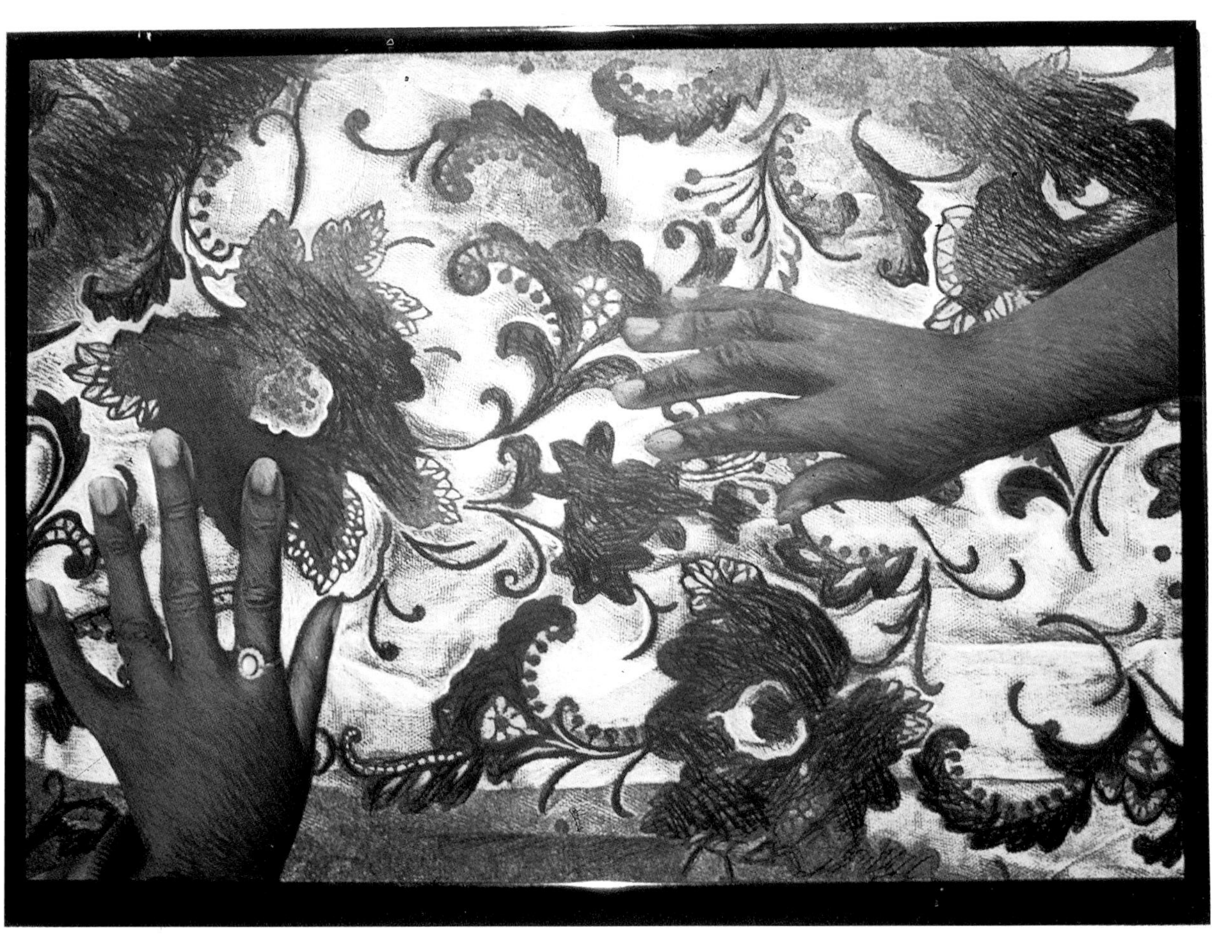

Conversational Piece:
Kitchen Table Talk, Strange Dreams 1986
mixed media on photograph

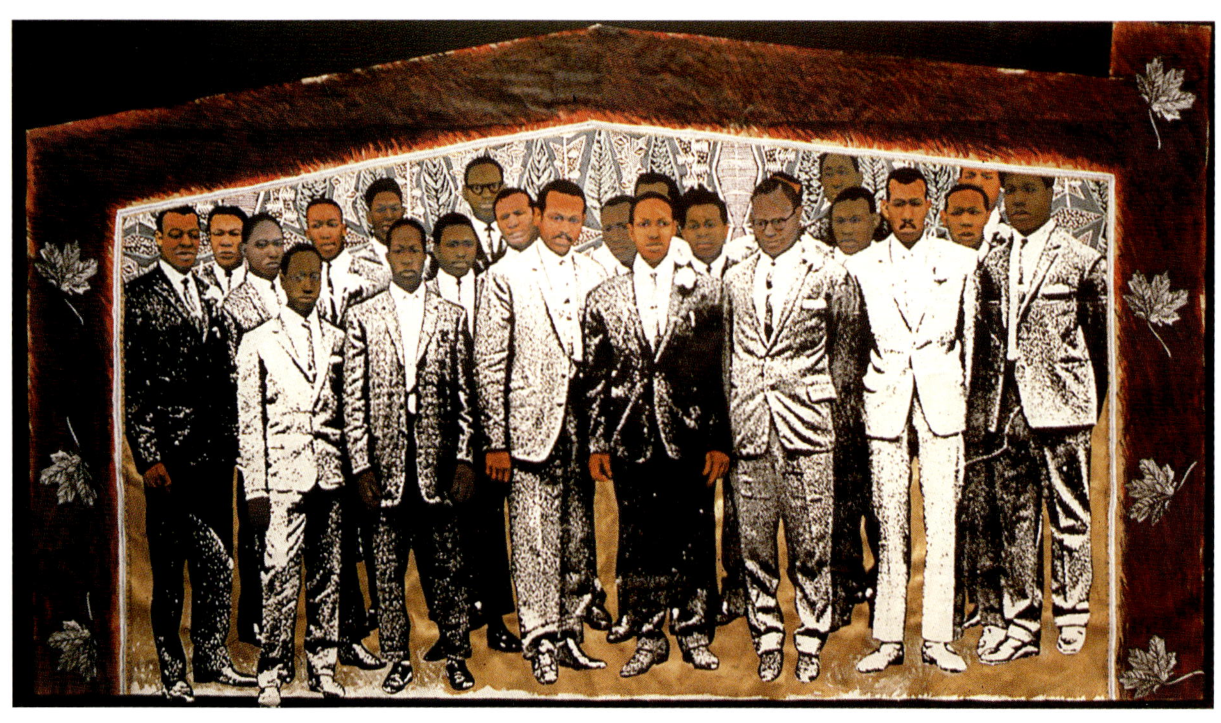

**Cricket Days   Domino Nights young arrivals/new home/homeless.
The streets are paved with gold in this green and pleasant land** 1986
pastels on photocopy

appearance of everyday things but at the same time they declare themselves to be fabricated images. They are not substitutes or facsimiles of the real but rather self-conscious reconstructions of reality which, in turn, reflect the subjects' own re-constructions of themselves as Boyce makes explicit in her title – *Auntie Enid – the Pose*. Boyce's images intertwine with the text of their titles, underlining both the constructed nature of what appears, to be real and also the gulf between expectation and reality in the experience of a whole generation of black people who emigrated to Britain from the Caribbean throughout the 1950s and in the early 1960s: *Cricket Days? Domino Nights! young arrivals/new home/homeless. The streets are paved with gold in this green and pleasant land.* In many ways, these works may be seen to be in dialogue with a catalogue of 'real' photographs which appeared as photo-stories in news magazines of the time like *Picture Post* and of which Stuart Hall has written eloquently:

> These shots were taken at the big London rail-stations, where the steamers spewed out their human cargo at the end of their long journeys – Kingston via Southampton, Avonmouth-Bristol and Liverpool docks, then by steam-train through the English rural and urban-industrial heartland, to Paddington, Victoria and Waterloo… People, dressed up to the nines, formally, for 'travelling' and even more, for 'arrival'. Wearing that expectant look – facing the camera, open and outward, into something they cannot yet see… the new life… just before you step off the end of the earth into… Britain, the ingrained, embattled nature of whose racism you do not yet know… because it hasn't yet hit you between the eyes… liminal movement caught between two worlds, hesitating on the brink.[4]

The gulf between the hopeful expectations of a new life conveyed in the clothes and demeanour of newly-arrived immigrants and the gloomy reality of racism, over-priced accommodation and low-paid jobs which awaited them was described by Sam Selvon in his novel *The Lonely Londoners*. Published in 1956, this contemporary novel draws on different dialects, syntaxes and vocabularies to create a complex, narrative composition about West Indian immigrant life in the 1950s which finds its visual parallel in Boyce's pastel drawings.

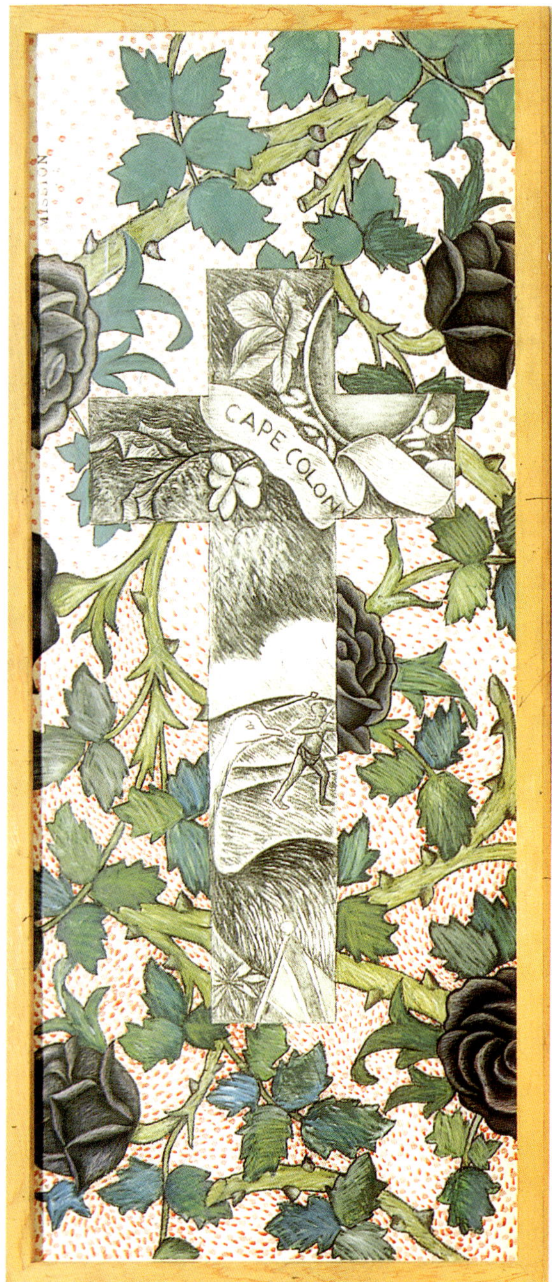

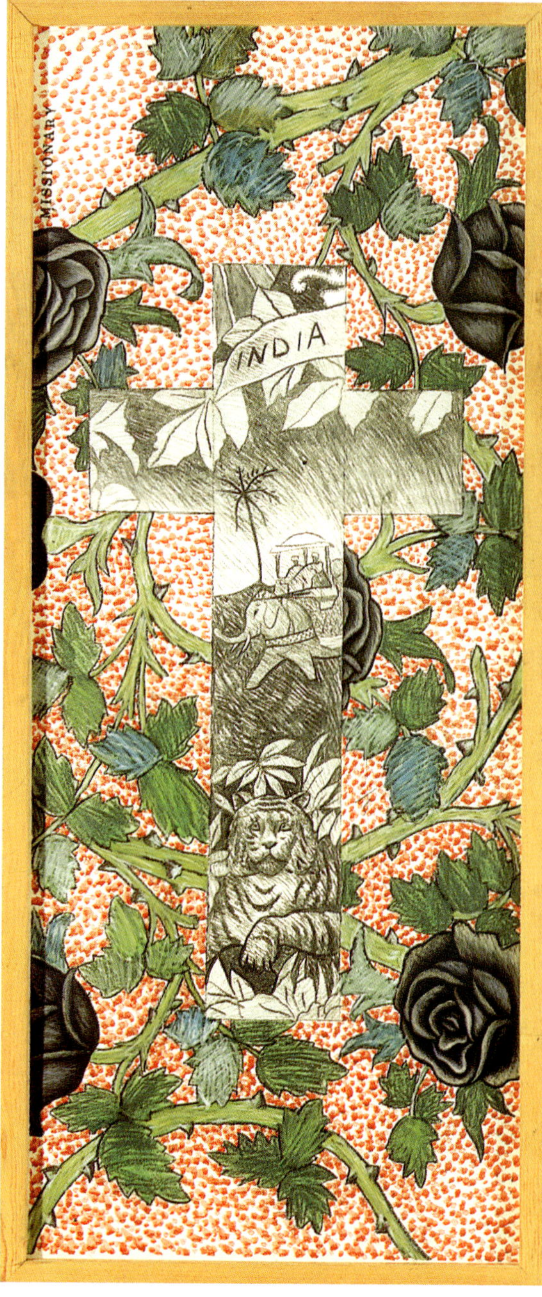

**Lay Back, Keep Quiet And Think Of What Made
Britain So Great** 1986
pastels on paper

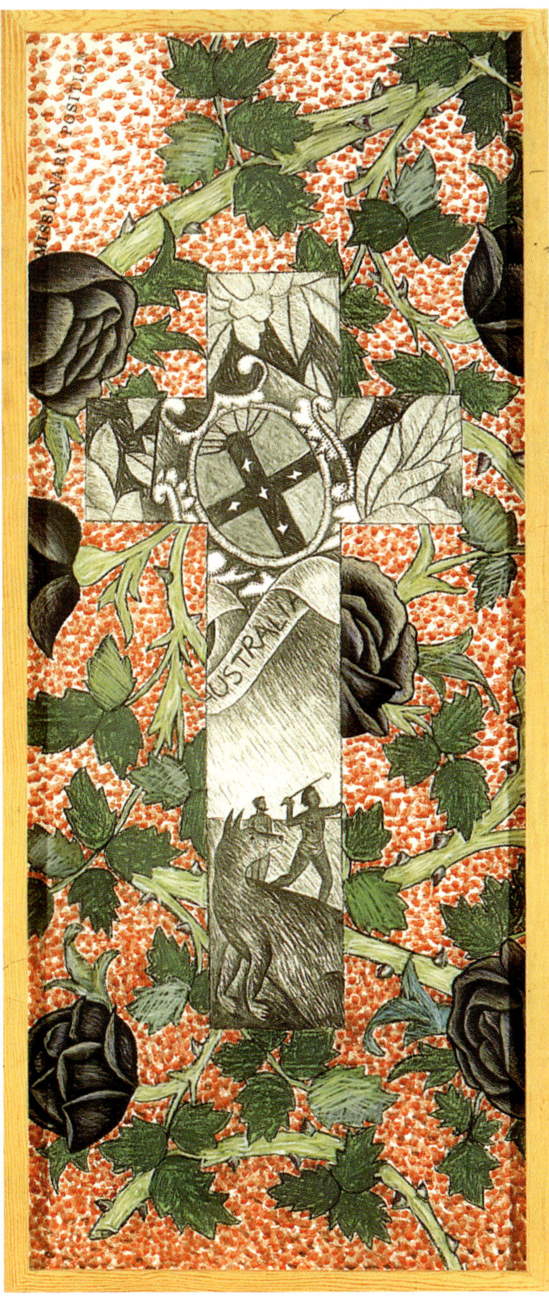
MISSIONARY POSITION
AUSTRALIA

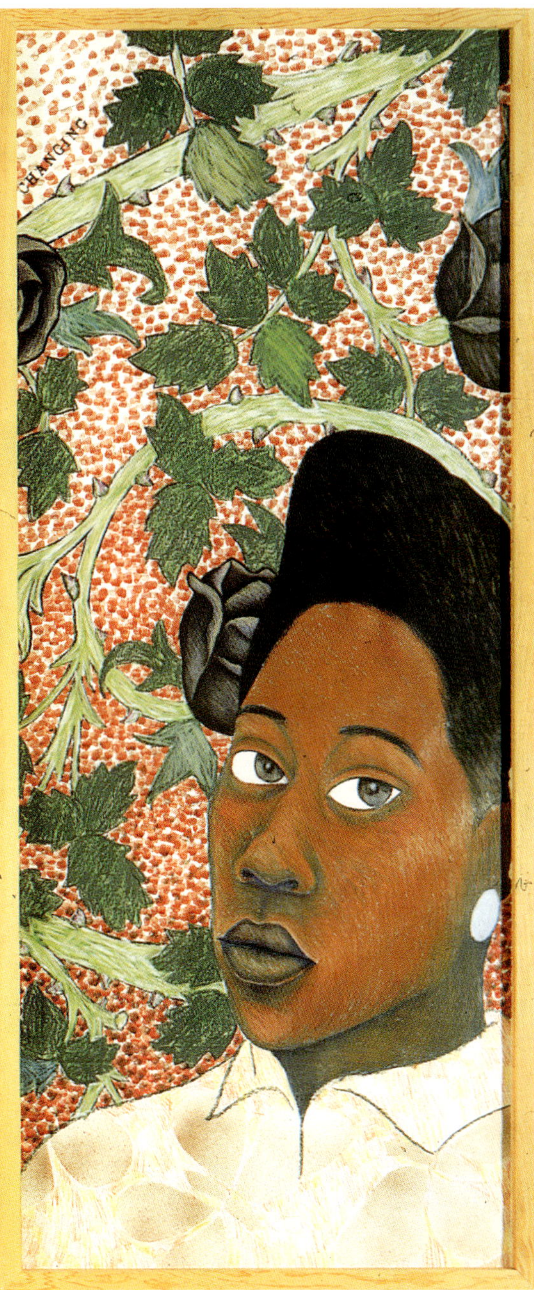
CHANGING

But while Selvon's novel documents the experience of his generation, Boyce's drawings carry an additional layer which may be described in Stuart Hall's words as the 'inflections on the image', the marks imprinted over a memory or representation by another period or, in this case, another generation. Just as Boyce has quite literally inscribed with pastels the surface of the photocopy in *Cricket Days? Domino Nights!* so she inscribes the memory and experience of her parent's generation with the readings and inflections of her own generation. In the same way that *The Lonely Londoners* is not a literal document of the experience of real people but a fictional account which draws on real experience, linguistic phrasing and so on, Boyce's drawings too do not document real lives but rather represent past memories and experiences which have been mediated and transformed by the artist in the present.

In *Conversational Piece* – another large mixed media work made in the same year as *Cricket Days? Domino Nights!* – a richly patterned tablecloth dominates the picture plane evoking stories from another place and time which envelop people and objects in the present. The hands of a black woman stand out against the cloth. Suspended above the table in 'freeze-frame', it is not clear whether these hands are about to smooth down the contours of the cloth against the table, or pull the cloth away leaving the table bare. Pushed flat against the picture plane, these anonymous hands seem to invite the viewer into the domestic space of the picture and at the same time exclude them from it. As elsewhere in Boyce's work, the designs of the past decorate the present and the relationship between past and present is always ambivalent and tenuous:

My use of pattern owes a lot to my mother's house: your eyes can't stop blinking for all the patterns in the house. When you go in the living room there are patterns everywhere, on the carpet, on the curtains, on the wallpaper, on the ceiling. They have their own co-ordination. When I started doing drawings about my childhood, I found a book on Fifties design, and I began to use some of the designs as backgrounds. It was at this point that I realised I was including my mother's influence, or rather a West Indian sense of decoration. The patterns though aren't simply there to decorate, but are there to give clues to the picture. Many of the images I produce are reminiscent of

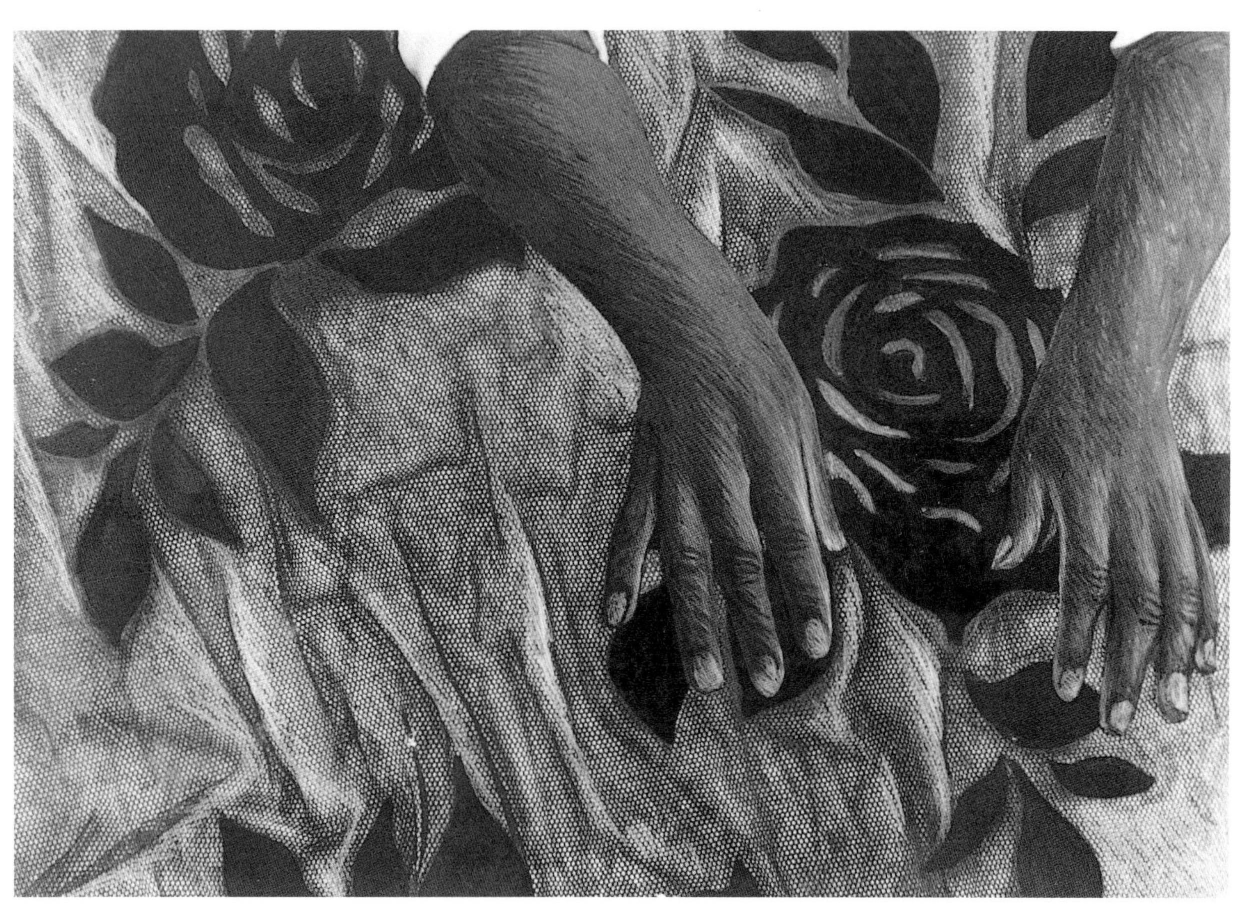

Bringing Up Babies 1986
mixed media on photograph

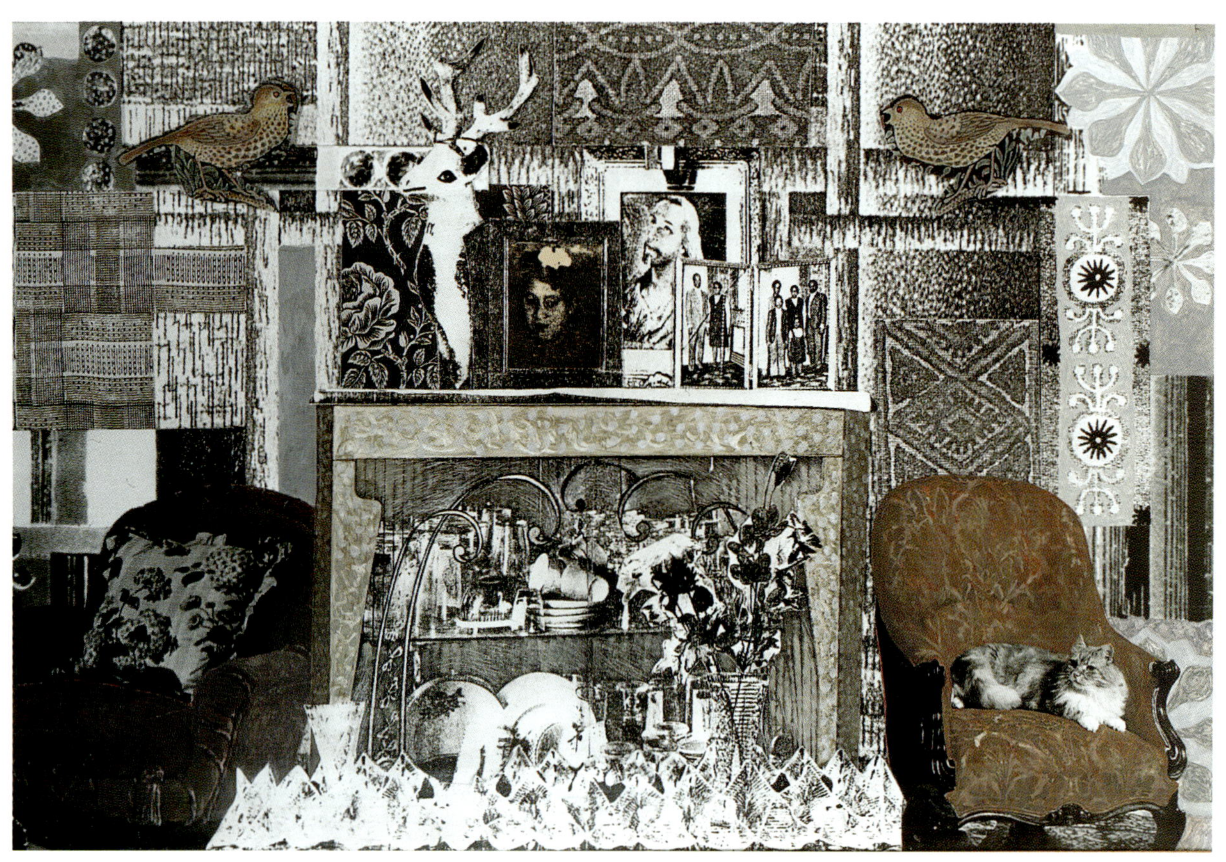

Interior 1988
mixed media on photograph

strip cartoons, snapshots etc., in that the image focuses, is edited down, to the essential information required. Rather than allowing the viewer into a pictorial/mirrored space, the created space is flattened, denying entry, yet often the figures depicted do invite entry. These contradictions between invitation, surface barrier and the sensuality of pastels and crayons is only something I have realised recently.[5]

The possibility of presenting narratives which are not linear or chronological and which break with the logic of sequential movements across space and time is explored in a number of Boyce's drawings. Works like *She Ain't Holdin' Them Up* and *Lay Back, Keep Quiet and Think of What Made Britain So Great (1986)* seem to defy their circumscribed domain. They are drawings but they are not in any way preparatory sketches for subsequent paintings. They are figurative works, apparently depicting 'real' people in 'real' space and time; and yet, the boundaries of 'real' space and time are consistently transgressed. Extending the conventional bounds of a triptych into a four-panel work, *Lay Back, Keep Quiet* is located at the intersection of diverse but related histories and cultures. Boyce has appropriated and transformed a wallpaper design originally conceived as a tribute to the fiftieth year of Queen Victoria's reign. Here as elsewhere in her work, the artist has adapted the nineteenth century wallpaper patterns of William Morris whose Victorian designs were among the first to attempt to 'picture' Englishness in purely visual terms. An avid collector of different patterns and materials, Boyce keeps these designs in a constant 'state of readiness' which are then transformed for use in her work:

> Collections of wallpaper designs, patterns and material, they tell stories. I start with an image in my head. As I begin to draw, the image changes, becomes modified, focused. There is a lot of censorship in my painting at a conscious level. Sometimes dreams help. What I suppress by day forces itself onto my consciousness by night, stubbornly painting itself on my canvas.[6]

While Morris' self-consciously nationalistic designs adopted the indigenous flora of the English countryside to promote an essentially

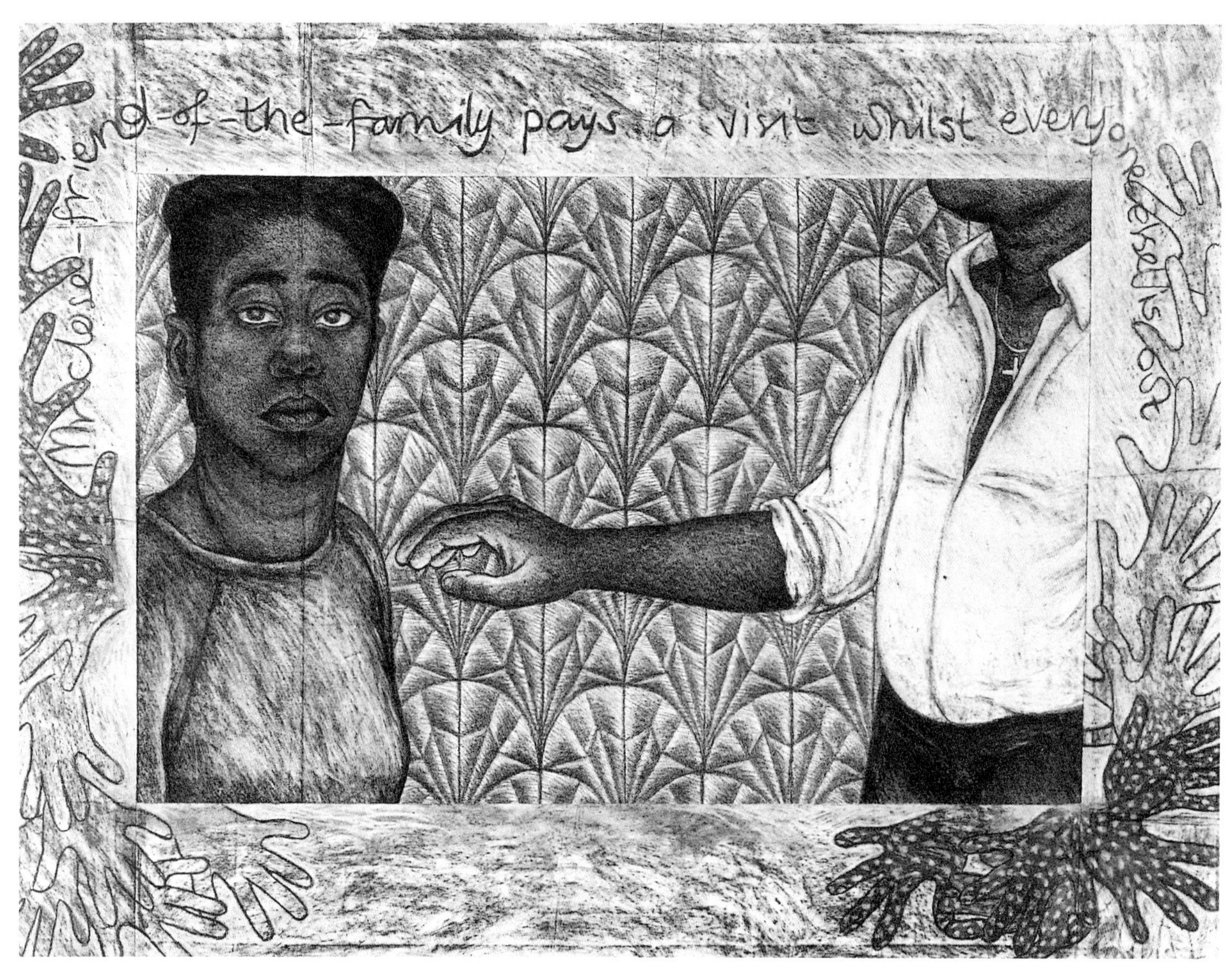

**Mr-Close-Friend-Of-The-Family Pays A Visit Whilst
Everyone Else Is Out** 1985
charcoal on paper

English iconography, Boyce has employed his designs to question the very notion of Englishness. The red rose and symbol of British nationhood which appeared in the original wallpaper has been usurped by a black rose which is present in every frame. The equivocal nature of the rose, whose fragility and beauty is combined with the sharpness and intractability of its thorns, becomes a metaphor for the ambivalence not only of 'Britishness' but also of 'blackness' and of femininity. Britain's imperial and colonial past is embedded in the decorative paper but so too is the resistance of native South Africans and Australians whose figures are just perceptible. The black woman who stares out at us from the final panel – a self-portrait of the artist herself – inherits a history of resistance as well as a history of oppression, that is, separate histories but ones which at the same time are locked together inextricably. According to Boyce, history is not something which lies 'out there' in dusty tomes, buried beneath the weight of the past. Rather, history envelops everyday life like the designs which paper our walls: the lives of individuals and the narratives of nation intersect just as do the realms of public and private life. Inscribed in the corners of the four panels are four words: Mission – Missionary – Missionary Position – Changing. Far from being fixed or static, these words shift subtly from frame to frame, inclining gently with the bough of the black rose. The artist seems to be suggesting that history and historical relationships are subject to change from within the very frame of representation. But she is also saying something about the nature of language and representation itself: that signs and meanings are subject to continuous transformation which confound a fixed, linear trajectory.

She Ain't Holdin' Them Up and *Lay Back, Keep Quiet and Think of What Made Britain So Great* mark a turning point in the artist's use of language. From the mid-80s onwards, the titles of Boyce's works became longer and longer – for example, *Mr-Close-Friend-Of-The-Family Pays A Visit Whilst Everyone Else Is Out* (1985) and *She Ain't Holding Them Up – She's Holding On (Some English Rose)* (1986) while text played an increasingly prominent role both inside and outside the frame of the image. Often witty and ironic, Boyce's titles played on the possibility of multiple and divergent readings of her work and the text within the frame introduced a range of voices into the works – the narrator, the protagonist, the 'chorus' and so on. Nowhere is this cacophony of voices more resonant than in

The *Essential Black Art* exhibition, curated by Rasheed Araeen was a serious attempt to historicise contemporary black art practice. (1988)

The *Impossible Self* was an exhibition curated by Sandy Nairne and Bruce Ferguson, which toured in Canada. It included the work of Raymonde April, Klaus vom Bruch, Miriam Cahn, Francesco Clemente, Anthony Gormley, Astrid Klein, Avis Newman and Jana Sterbak. (1988)

The Other Story, although an excellent and overdue exhibition, spelt the end of big black survey shows. Again, there were many public and private disputes about this exhibition. The media coverage on the one hand, and the absence of work by any Asian women artists on the other.
(1989)

Missionary Position I (1985) where hand-written text is interlaced into the background design and is barely legible with the exception of quotations from the Bible which are set off against a vivid, pink background. The dissonant voices which vie with one another in *Missionary Position I* echo the intimate relationship between religious and colonial hegemony in Britain's former colonies whose legacy continues into the present.

'*Missionary Position I*

lay back

Our Father who art in Heaven...

As children my mother would recite the Lord's prayer with us at bedtime

Hallowed be thy name

in command and control

<u>Them that's got shall get</u>
<u>Them that's not shall hate</u>

I was really proud when I received a copy of Gideon's Bible at school

Total submission'

In *Lay Back, Keep Quiet* the text within the frame not only forms part of the entire pictorial design of the image but moves the use of text from the descriptive and the narrative to the pictorial. To put it another way, the words Mission – Missionary – Missionary Position – Changing metamorphose from frame to frame, functioning as pictograms in this work, effectively eliding the distinction between word and image, and between visual narrative and linguistic narrative. In her longest titled work *From Tarzan to Rambo: English Born 'Native' Considers Her Relationship to the <u>Constructed</u> Image and her Self* of 1987, Boyce goes further incorporating existing images, materials and

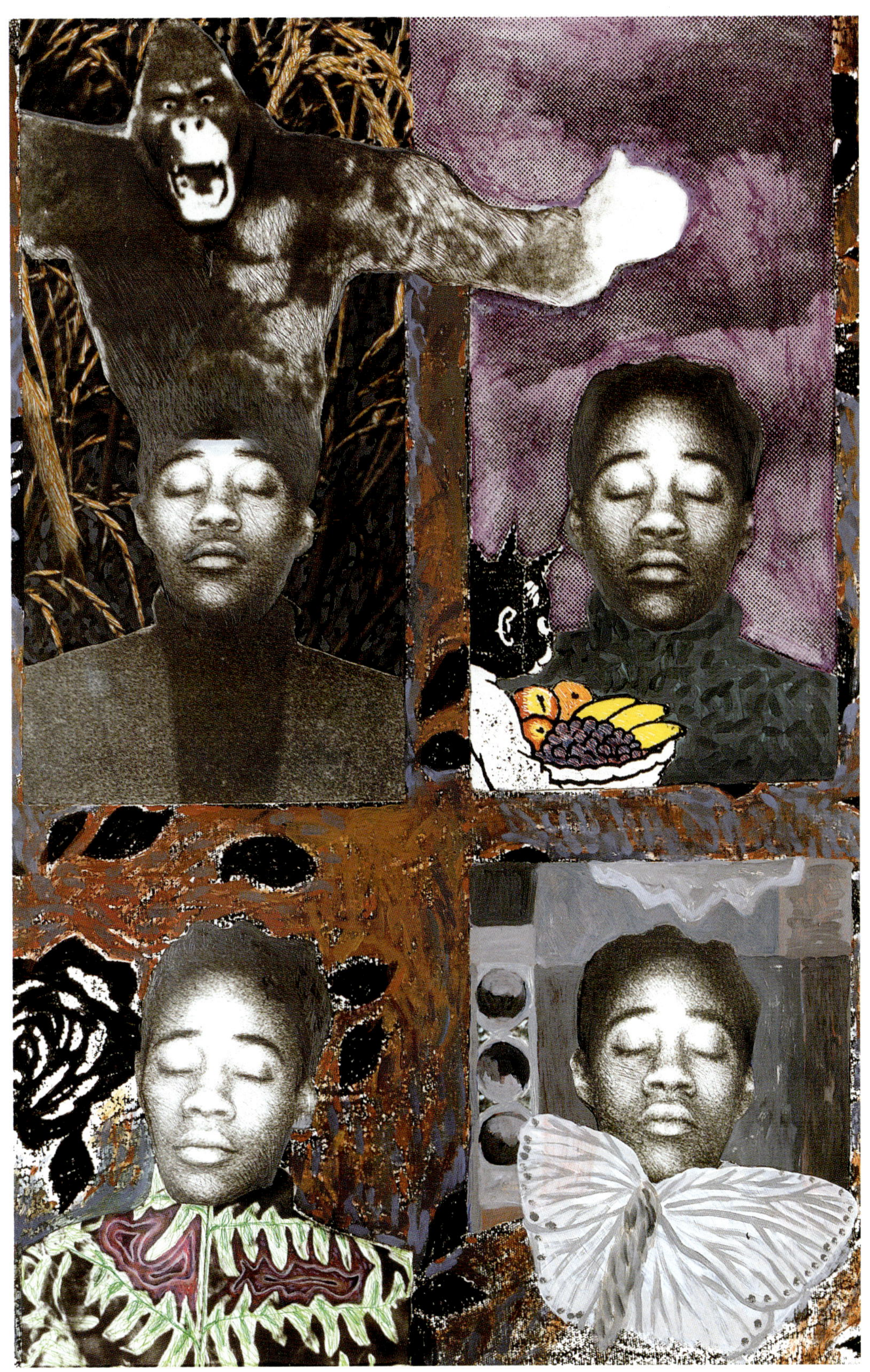

From Someone Else's Fear Fantasy To Metamorphosis 1987
Mixed media on photograph

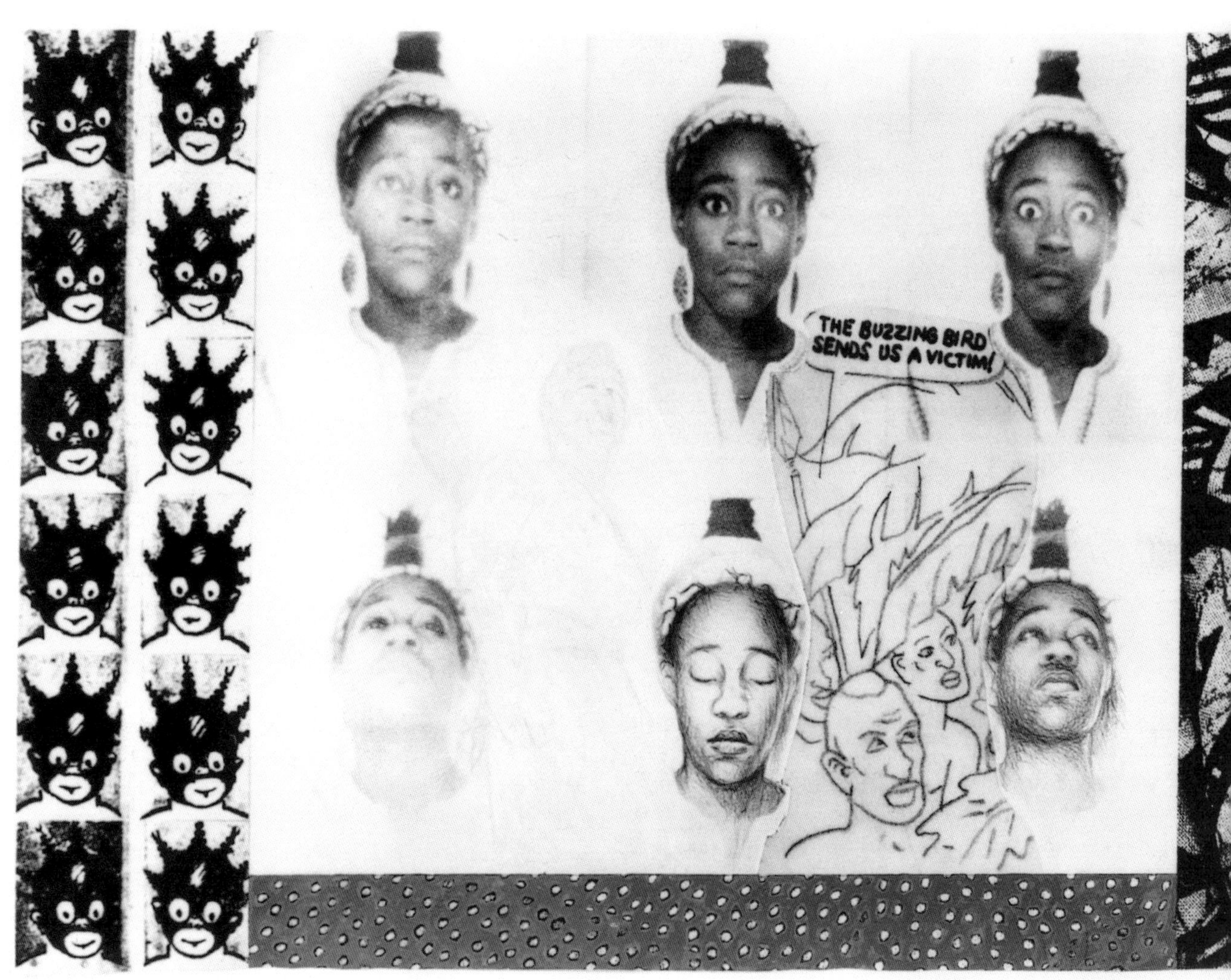

From Tarzan To Rambo: English Born 'Native' Considers Her Relationship To The <u>Constructed</u> Image And Her Roots In Reconstruction 1987
Self
mixed media on photograph

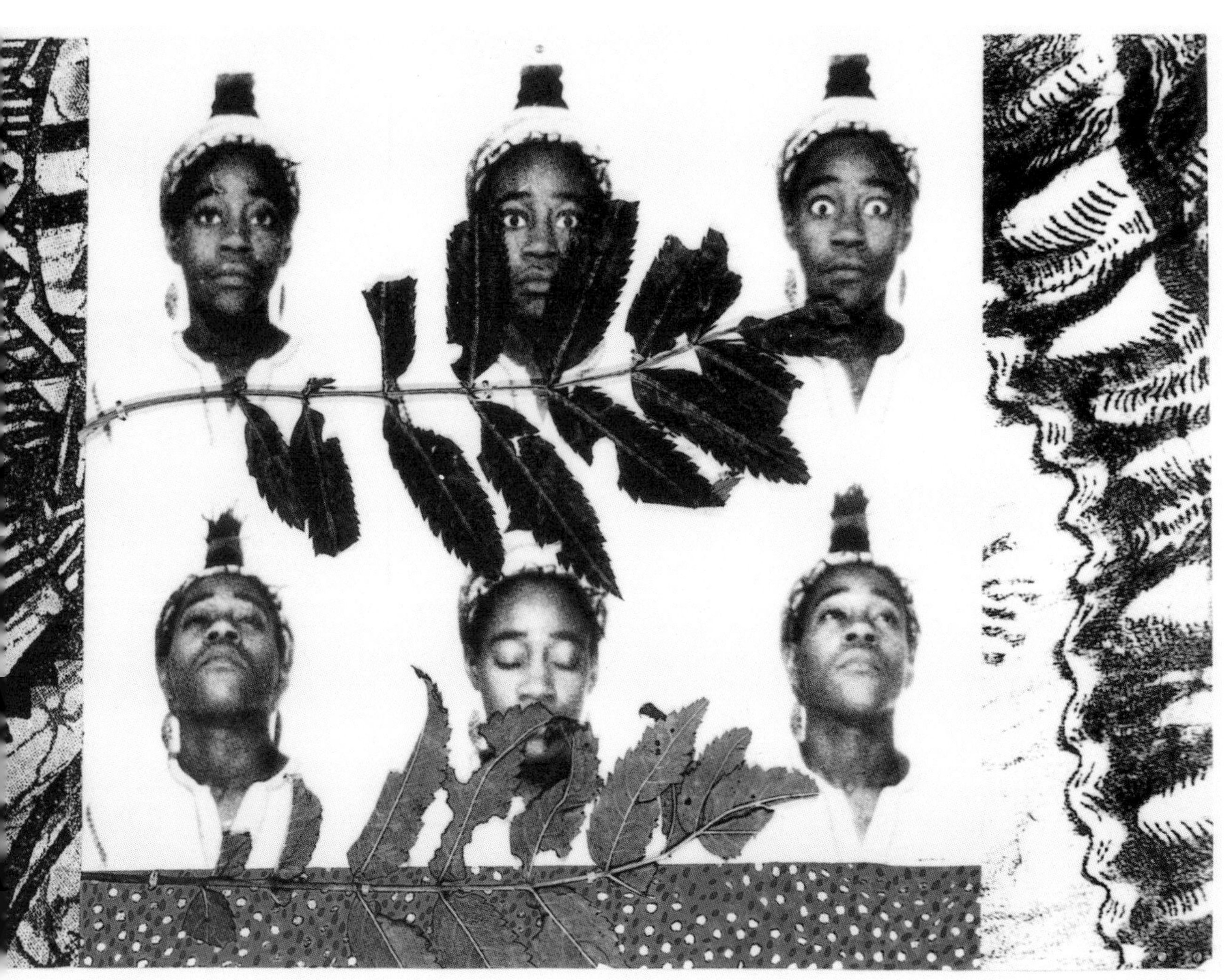

objects into the frame and exploring the fragile line which demarcates fictional representation and self-representation, the media image and self-image. *From Tarzan to Rambo* was made shortly after *She Ain't Holdin Them Up* and signalled Boyce's move away from her early pastel drawings to experimentation with other media and artistic processes which included photography, photocopy and collage. In place of wallpaper designs, Boyce here draws on a collection of photocopies culled from comics and magazines. For Boyce, the process of collecting seems to mirror the process of memory where fragments of everyday life are set aside and stored, to be re-used, re-collected at a later date. Like memories, these fragments are mediated both by the selectivity of the collector and by the action of the collector on these fragments which have been photocopied, re-assembled and then drawn upon by the artist. As always in Boyce's work, there is a fine line between form and content, between the meaning of the work and the artistic means which have been deployed to communicate that meaning. The individual visual elements which make up *From Tarzan to Rambo* − photobooth portraits of the artist, cartoon 'gollywogs', comic book images of Tarzan and 'native' tribes people, African cloth and leaves − have been mediated and circum-scribed by the artist's hand (they have been assembled, re-pho-tographed and drawn upon), in the same way that representations of black people have been fixed in negative stereotypes and effectively 'framed' by the very processes which represent and mediate their image in popular culture whether through comics (*Rupert the Bear* and *Terrifying Tales* from the 1920s and 1950s respectively) or Hollywood movies (the Tarzan films, produced from 1918 onwards; *King Kong* (1933); *I Walked With a Zombie* (1943); *Rambo: First Blood Part II* (1985)).[7] The massive scale of the piece self-consciously evokes the cinema screen and draws heavily on the artist's interest and critical reading of American cinema and its reconstruction of black people for consumption by both black and white audiences. As in *Lay Back, Keep Quiet* and *Missionary Position I*, Boyce draws a thread between seemingly disparate domains:

I had been doing a lot of reading round religion and African influences in Christianity and there's a ceremonial aspect to Black church which is about 'getting the spirit' and talking in tongues… at church you can get into a particular state where

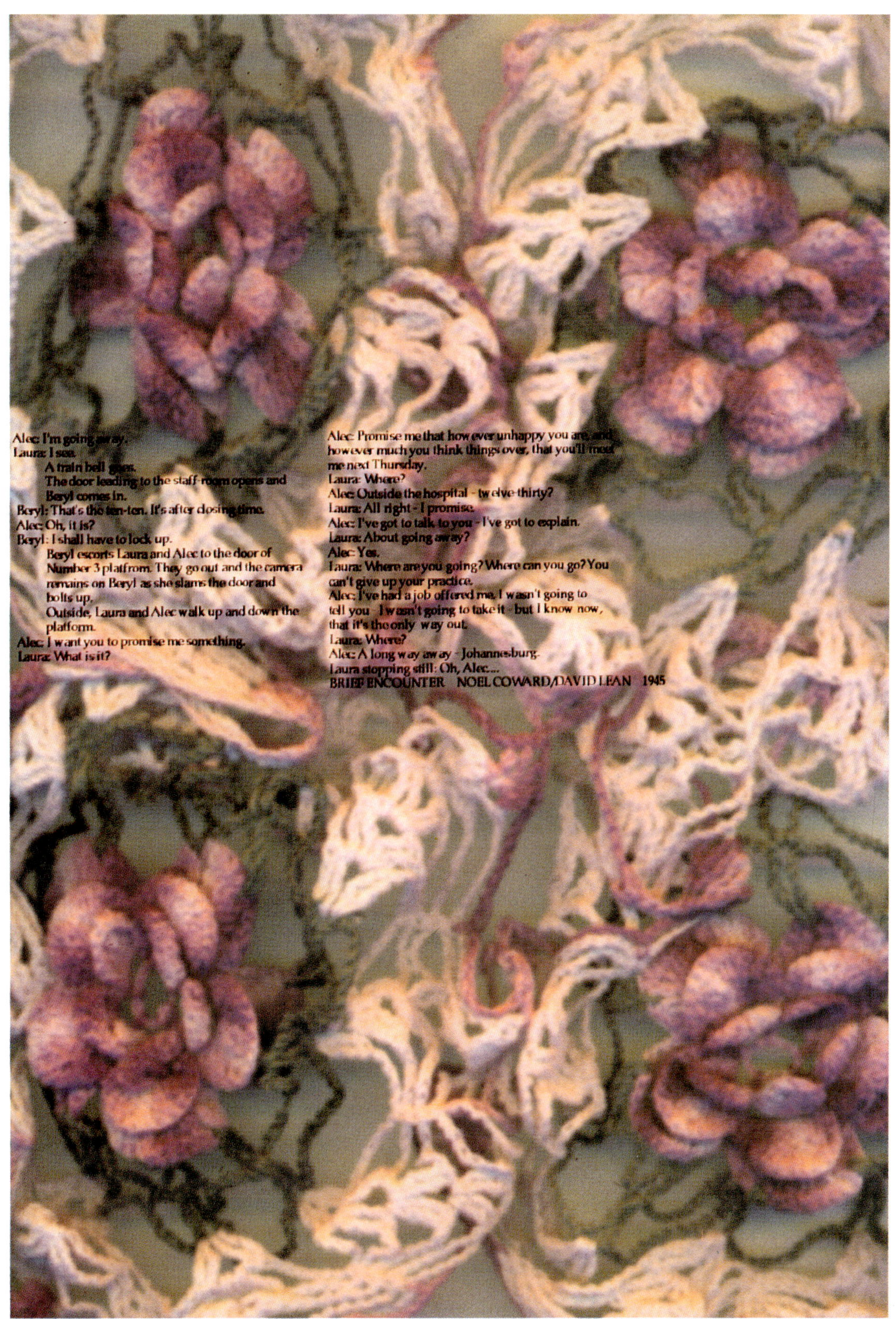

4 Tablecloths 1992
image and text printed on vinyl

your eyes roll because you get into another level. I realised that what was going on in those films was a parody of what was going on in the church… That's only part of it. I started to think about this whole thing about black people being an audience to media reconstruction of that, and internalising, and having to find other alternatives.[8]

Film, film narrative, and the role of audience in relation to a film's narrative have preoccupied Boyce over the past decade. Works like *From Tarzan to Rambo* clearly owe a great deal to the artist's engagement with Hollywood movies and film theory during this period. In the same year, Boyce worked with the film-maker Martina Attille on her influential short film *Dreaming Rivers* for which Boyce designed the sets.

In Boyce's wall-based works from the mid and late '80s, the picture frame seems to operate in the same way as the single frame of a moving picture. It delineates a fragment suspended in space and time, a moment in time rather than 'a whole story', mirroring the snippets of conversation overheard within the family as well as the pre-migratory memories of home, family and friends which assume a magical and immutable status in the imagination of most migrants. Nostalgic longing for an irrecoverable past provides the focus for a later installation work commissioned in 1992 from Sonia Boyce by Camden Arts Centre as part of the public art project Northern Adventures, located in St. Pancras Station in north London. The *4 Tablecloths* (1992) piece, which interweaves three different narratives, one fictional, the other two apparently factual, speaks of desire and disjuncture in the lives of three women from different classes, races and generations whose paths cross in the tea-shop of a railway station. To create the installation, Boyce fabricated four tablecloths to cover the tables of the British rail tea-rooms at St. Pancras station. The artist was attracted to the environment of the tea-rooms which were 'so artificially cosy yet sterile and dated'. The tea-rooms are the quintessential transitory space, what Boyce describes as a 'perfect kind of ante-chamber for all the hustle and bustle of a busy station', which mediates private and public space, stillness and movement, departing and arriving. Each tablecloth, made from vinyl-coated polyester, is imprinted with the same image of a floral, embroidered design but inscribed with different texts.

Extracts from the dialogue of the two protagonists of David Lean's classic film *Brief Encounter* (1945) is intertwined with the narratives of two black women: a 'semi-retired West Indian Christian lady' and a young Asian woman, both of whom are anticipating imminent encounters: a 'blind date' due to arrive on a train from Derby in the case of the former, and a job interview in Nottingham in the case of the latter. As in earlier works like *Missionary Position I*, the voices of different characters mingle with each other in a space which remains, characteristically of Boyce, neither a fictional nor a real space, neither private nor public, but a space where such subtle distinctions become eroded and where individual desires are within a whisker's breadth of becoming real possibilities:

Semi-retired West Indian Christian lady, seeks religious unattached gentlemen for sincere relationship. Leading to nuptials. Genuine replies only. Write to Box 961B.

My crazy children put me up to this 'Come on mum you need a bit of excitement in your life'. Well here I am waiting for the 3.15 from Derby, I hope I don't miss the announcement for the platform – it's so noisy in here. I wonder if Trevor's as nice as his letters. I should have worn the pale blue dress-suit instead, Oh! this is silly – he's only coming down to spend the day with my family, nothing to get het up about… I feel like a young girl courting for the first time.[9]

Importantly for Boyce, the space of the railway station tea-room is also a transgressive one which allows the artist to explore 'the idea of an encounter between strangers in a public yet intimate space. For some it raises anxieties about safety, the known. It suggests a transgression, particularly for women – moving beyond acceptable behaviour – a sure sign of our modern age'.[10] Yet Boyce moves her work beyond the mildly transgressive content of the original film and the imminent moral and sexual transgression of its main characters Alec (Trevor Howard) and Laura (Celia Johnson). She does this by disrupting the narrative structure of the film in her own 're-staging' of the crucial 'first encounter' scene between Alec and Laura in the tea-room of a suburban railway station:

Most of the year is taken up with co-organising a memorial lecture of Rotimi Fani-Kayode along with his (now deceased) partner Alex Hirst and Michael Cadette.
(1990)

The *British Art Show* seems to promise the possibility of representing a new image of my work.
(1990)

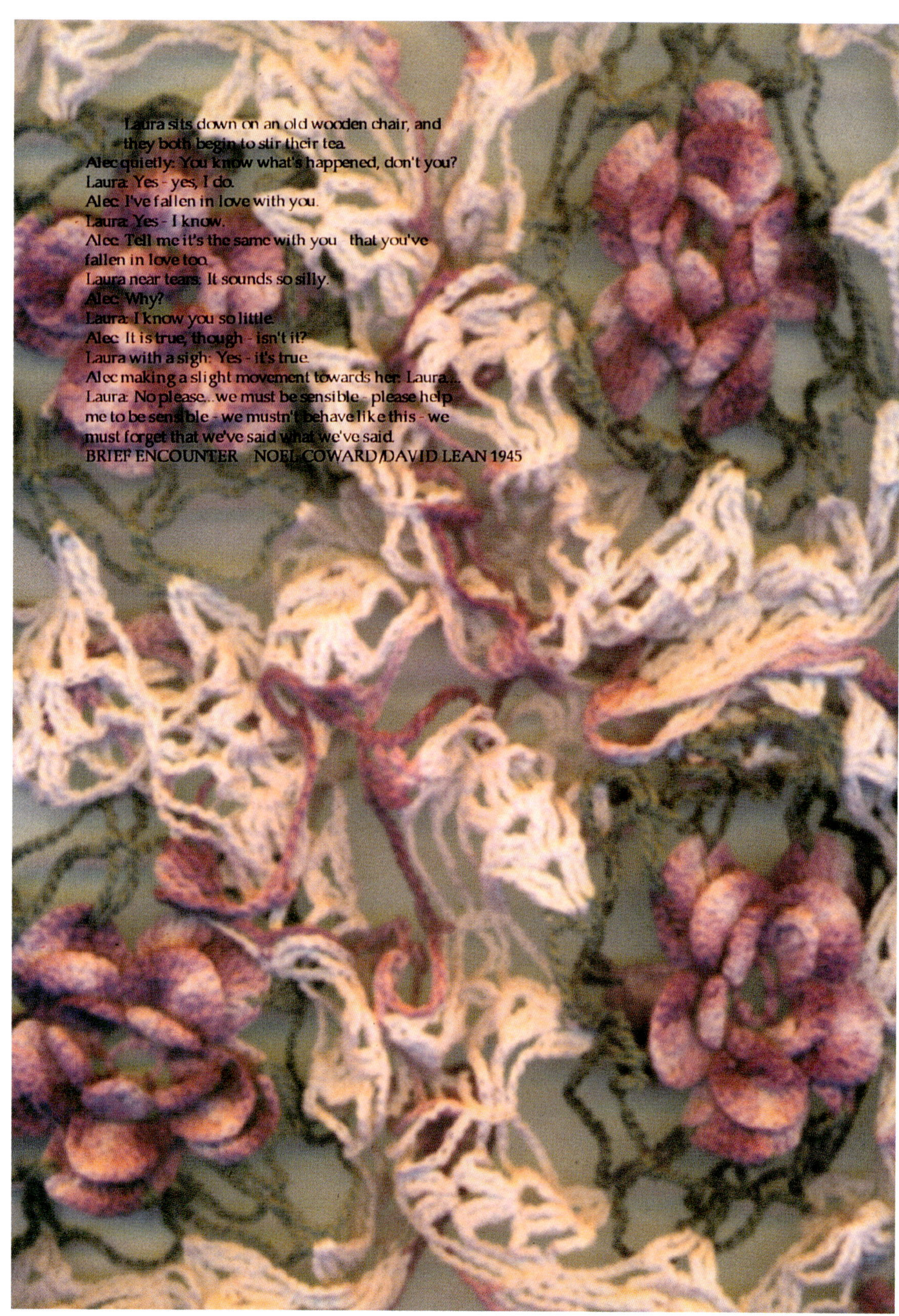

4 Tablecloths 1992
image and text printed on vinyl

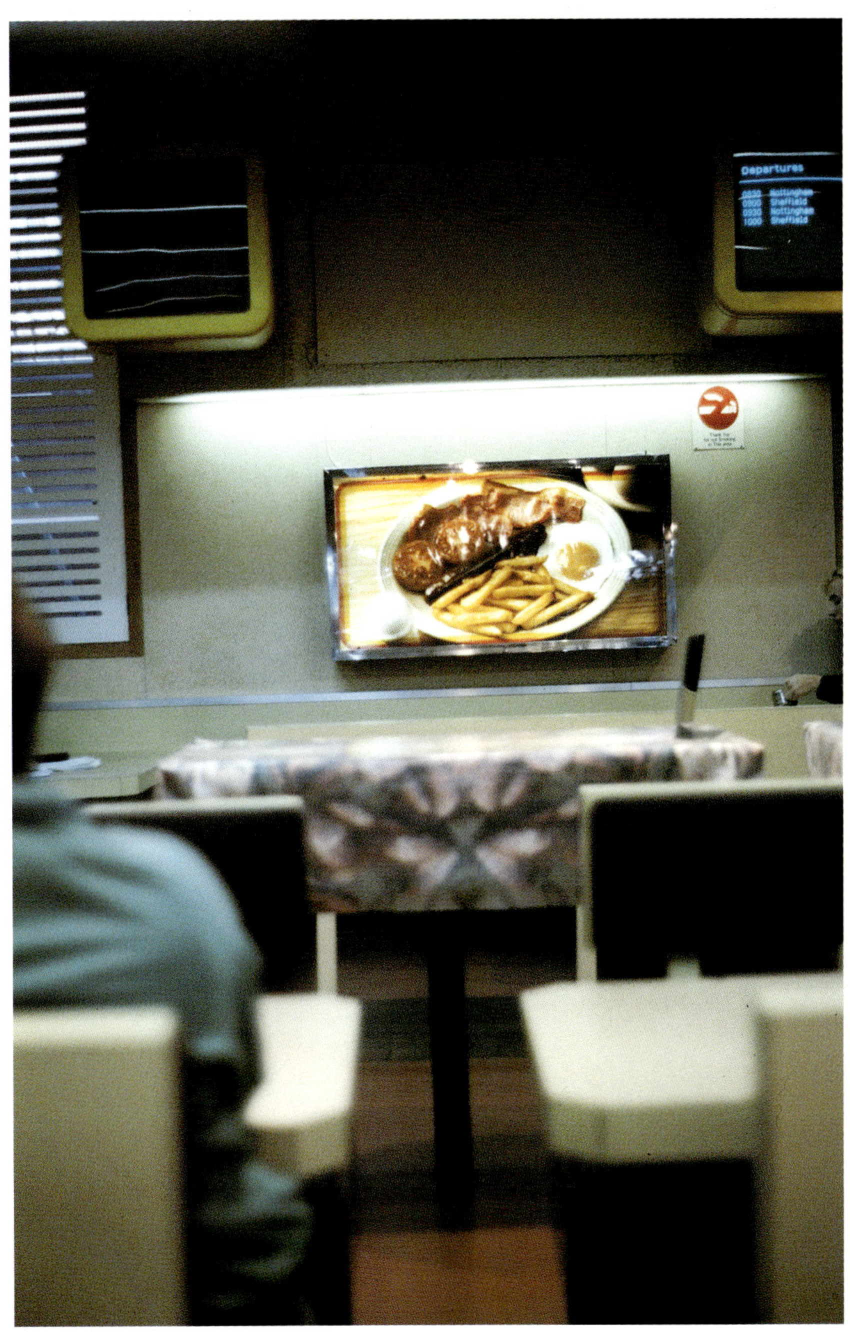

installation view of **4 Tablecloths** at St Pancras Station
Travellers Fare 1992

It had already been a mad panicky morning trying to get organised for the interview up in Nottingham…

1 ASIAN WOMAN SUPPORT WORKER
Must be fluent speaker and writer of Gujarati (section 5.2.d Race Relations Act and 7.2.b of the Sex Discrimination Act applies). The Support Worker must have the relevant professional qualifications and at least 1 year's experience of working with people in a residential context. Welfare rights knowledge and/or nursing background would be useful.

… with about half an hour to spare before the 8.30 left, I thought I'd have a cup of tea in the Traveller's Fare. Just my luck, there was a commotion going on at the food counter.

Rucksana: *Can I help?*

Alec: *Oh, no please – it's only something in my eye.*

Staff 1:   *Try pulling down your eyelid as far as it will go.*

Staff 2:   *And then blow your nose.*

Rucksana: *Please let me look. I happen to be a nurse.*

Alec: *It's very kind of you.*

Rucksana: *Turn around to the light please.*

As we got close I noticed how young and quite handsome he was.

Rucksana: *Now – look up – now look down – I can see it. Keep still… There.*

Alec (blinking): *Oh dear, what a relief – it was agonising.*

Rucksana: *It looks like a bit of grit.*

Alec: *It was. How lucky for me you were here.*

Rucksana: *Anybody could have done it.*

Alec: *Well you did, and I'm most grateful.*

Rucksana: *There's my train – good-bye.*[11]

The insertion of Rucksana, a young Asian woman into the text of this quintessential mid-1940s British film, not only disrupts the original text (which Boyce has consciously re-staged in a non-linear sequence across the four tablecloths which make up the work) but introduces a black protagonist into the film, and hence into post-war British culture. Just as a black rose usurps the place of William Morris' red rose in *Lay Back, Keep Quiet*, the tangential relationship of *Brief Encounter* to Britain's colonial past (towards the end of the film, Alec leaves England for Johannesburg) allows Boyce to inverse the colonial relationship within the very narrative of the film. Whereas Britain's former empire remains an absent presence in the film (Johannesburg is 'a long way away' as Alec tells Laura), the empire 'comes back' in Boyce's narrative to play a critical role in the 'real' story of Britain's past, present and future.

1   Homi K. Bhabha, 'Introduction', in Homi K. Bhabha (ed.) *Nation and Narration*, Routledge, London and New York, pp.1–4.

2   A conversation piece is a genre picture, traditionally consisting of two or more small portraits of people represented in appropriate surroundings, usually domestic. It is an informal group portrait and usually represents members of the same family.

3   Sonia Boyce, quoted in Sandy Nairne, *State of the Art: Ideas and Images in the 1980s*, Chatto & Windus, London, 1987, p.237.

4   Stuart Hall, 'Reconstruction Work', from *Critical Decade: Black British Photography in the 80s*, *Ten-8*, vol.2, no.3, Spring 1992.

5   Sonia Boyce from John Roberts, 'Interview with Sonia Boyce', *Third Text*, 1, Autumn 1987, pp.62–63.

6   Ibid. above.

7   For a detailed analysis of *From Tarzan to Rambo*, see Tate Gallery catalogue, entry no.T 05021. This work and a closely-related piece *From Someone Else's Fear Fantasy (A Case of Mistaken Identity, This is No Bed of Roses) To Metamorphosis* (1987) derives its structure in part from the Surrealist photomontage published in *La Révolution surréaliste* in 1929 which depicts portraits of the male Surrealist artists with their eyes closed, surrounding René Magritte's painting *La femme cachée* of the same year.

8   Ibid. above.

9   Text by Sonia Boyce from Table 1 of the installation *4 Tablecloths* (1992).

10   Sonia Boyce from 'Proposal for 4 Tablecloths', unpublished.

11   Text by Sonia Boyce from Table 1 of the installation *4 Tablecloths* (1992).

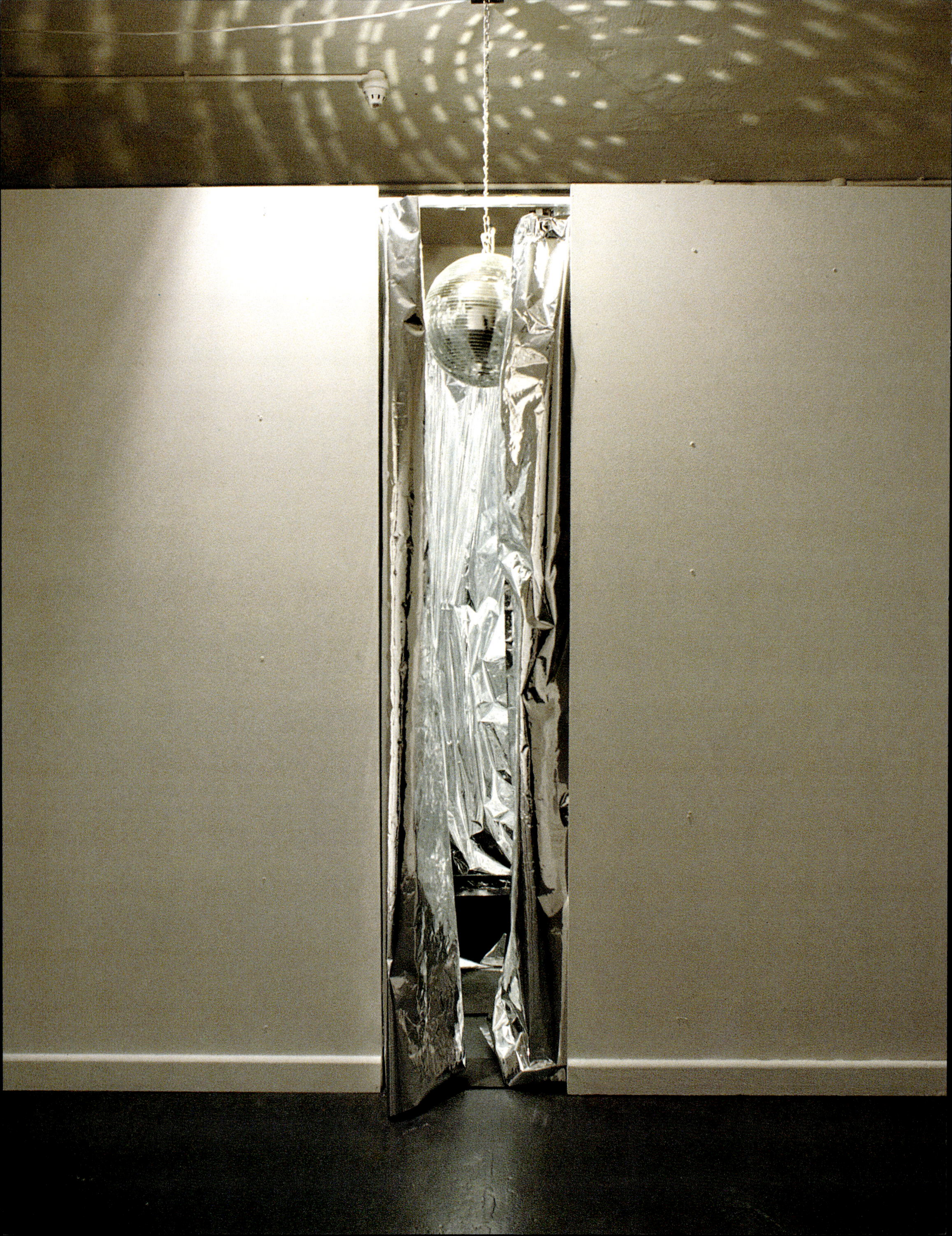

Modern Living

> With cities, it is with dreams: everything imaginable can be dreamed but even the most unexpected dream is a rebus that conceals a desire or, its reverse, a fear. Cities, like dreams are made of desires and fears, even if the thread of their discourse is secret, their rules absurd, their perspectives deceitful, and everything conceals something else.
>
> Italo Calvino, *Invisible Cities*[1]

In the late 1980s and early 1990s, Boyce's work became increasingly concerned with the intersection of private and public realms within the modern, urban environment. London, the quintessential post-colonial city, becomes both the stage and the central protagonist in Boyce's narratives of fear and desire which are refracted through the prism of the multi-racial metropolis of the late twentieth century. Whereas in earlier works like *Missionary Position II* (1985) Boyce had been preoccupied with domestic space as the arena in which the personal and political become fused together, in later works like the image and text piece *Underground* (1990), the artist explores the conjuncture of physical and mental space in the city and, most importantly for Boyce, the spaces which lie in-between its fixed geographical locations:

Underground

The shame of it guy.
Forgetting the distance between one step and another.
Tripping down the escalator. To ecstasy. Paranoia. Pain.
Faking longing. Reaching. Outstretched arms
of the law.
A victorious narrative disrupted by our presence.
Blunt instruments. Attack. Fire water. Anger.
Changing strategies. From actor to producer.
Could she master her own moods and movements.
Slowly rubbing. Drawing. Shape. Riding over the folds.
Take me. Rushing guilt. Faster.

Initiated into the world of digital technology at ARTEC. I received money from Impressions Gallery, and the London 2000 project to make work for the Photo Video exhibition. This involved a huge cast of people Models: Kethi Ngcobo, Ka-che Kwok, Franco Bossisso, Kimi Takesue and Ajamu Ikwe Tyehimba. Eddie George and Trevor Mathison from Black Audio Film Collective did the sound. Technical assistance in manipulating images and editing sequences on an Apple Mac through Joe Epstein and Charlotte Sexton. (1991)

Is It Love That You're After Or Just A Good Time 1992
miralon, rubber and mirror ball

Which way we going baby.
The doors opened. Victoria
station. Awake suddenly.
The crowds pushed and pulled their way in and out.
I am the enemy within.
They thought.
Simultaneously.
Policing silence.
Not knowing. We repeat the same pattern.
Cutting each other out. As other.
Aggressive. No noise. Smell. Perspiration and bowel ensemble to
Euston. Let's have an awayday.
Dreaming in glorious colour. Searching for shared routes.
Yet circuits disconnect and computers terminate along this journey to
my friends. Notice the insensitive. Social security. Secret
glances indirectly stolen. While travelling elusive.
Delusions grand.
Your wildest obsessions delight angels.
Turkish, Chinese, Indian, Latin American,
African. Carob and honey coated wholesome desire.
Designer doubt.
Something else off the therapy shelf. Consuming interest.
Spending time. Wasting money. Moving.
Highbury and Islington. Then on to the end of the line.[2]

In the large-scale mixed media work *Talking Presence* (1988), Boyce maps out another transitory space where her protagonists are suspended in an ambivalent zone between private and public spheres. Two naked, black figures – one male, one female – are silhouetted against the interior and exterior architecture of the city. They are neither inside nor outside, neither viewers nor participants in the spectacle of the capital whose multiple and often contradictory facets converge upon each other – the modern council block and the Georgian terraced house, the tourist icons (St. Pauls and the taxicab, the Houses of Parliament and red double-decker bus) and the graffiti-emblazoned walls of working-class districts. There is a tension too between the relentlessly urban exterior landscape and the configurations of the private space of this anonymous black couple whose mantelpiece bears traces of the sea and the countryside –

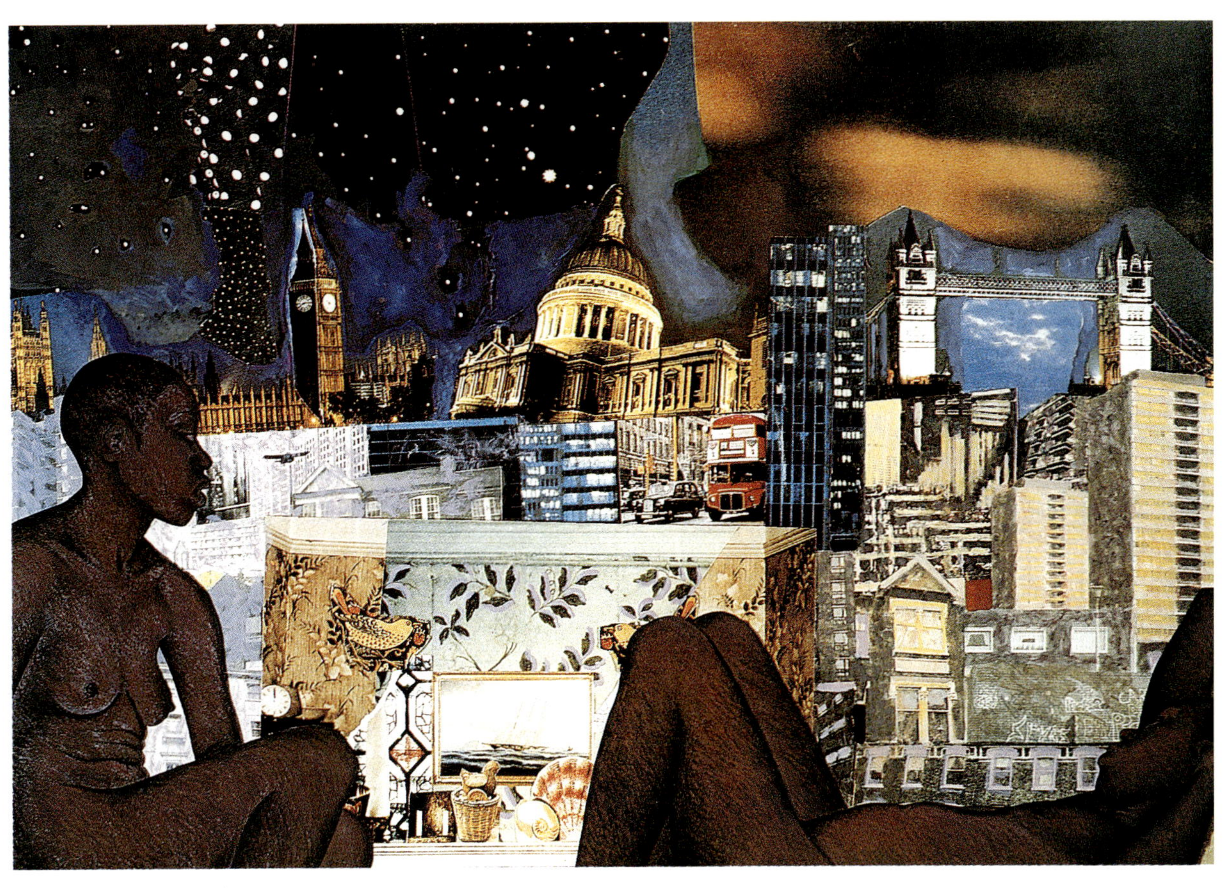

Talking Presence 1988
mixed media on photograph

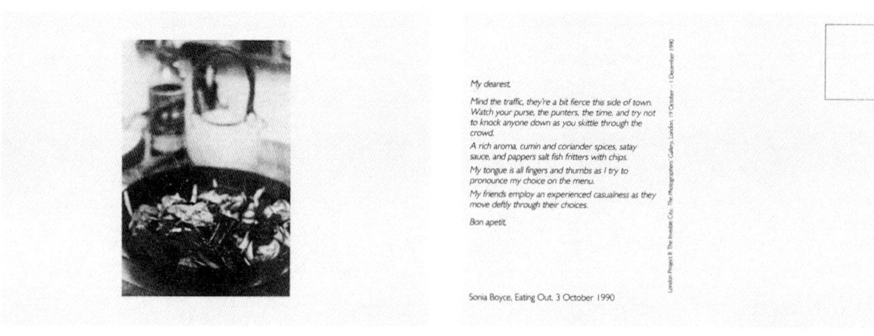

a) **Eating Out**

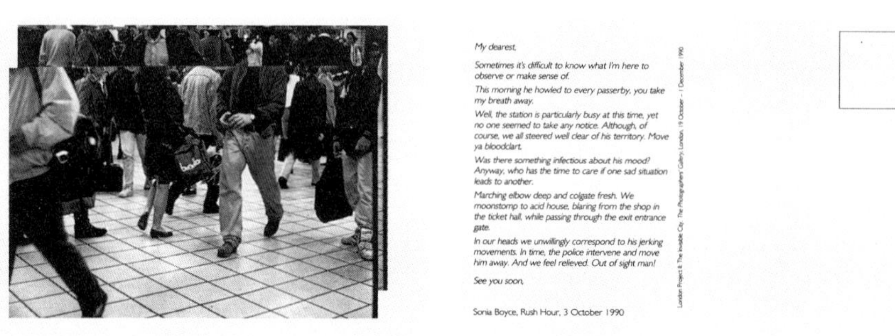

a) **Rush Hour**

The Ticket Machine 1990
6 postcards

shells, a painting of a ship on the high seas, wallpaper filled with birds and foliage – visual memorabilia of another place and another time which persist in mediating individual, black experience in the metropolis.

As Boyce's images moved away gradually from the strong figurative and hand-drawn elements of her earlier works to include collage, photography and installation, long narrative texts like *Underground* (1990) frequently accompanied her images or were integrated into the fabric of the work. Through both image and text, the artist sought 'to articulate the language of modernity and urban life' and the ways in which 'technology, architectural spaces, the media mediates human contact'.[3] All these elements came together in two installation works commissioned from Boyce for an exhibition held at The Photographers' Gallery in 1990 entitled *The Invisible City*. Continuing her interrogation of the individual's relationship to the city, Boyce re-created two familiar structures from the cityscape – *the photobooth* and *the ticket machine* – whose equivocal functions lie somewhere between the public and the private, the individual and the communal, the intimate and the exposed:

> Boyce's photobooth is an ambiguous marker in London's feverish competition for space, a structure in which implied extremes of scale are forced into uneasy conjunction. Its mirrored surface gleams like a building from London's new incandescent cityscape, and yet it is visibly a room for one. The interior, decorated with a patchwork of softly delineated domestic imagery, is a haven of comfort and reassurance but one in which freedom of movement is denied. The viewer/visitor is constrained to a fixed position as if in a cell. Referred to by the artist as 'a space for the homeless', the photobooth is an image – a home, crowded with irony and contradiction. The ticket machine also offers conflicting signs and messages, but they are written down – printed in the form of postcards and dispensed at the push of a button. The various cards represent an ability to choose… the city of possibilities – and the promise of human contact. Routes and situations are suggested, described, but there are restrictions and complications, we are caught in a confusion of entrances, exits and no go areas, following divergent streams of consciousness.[4]

Making the *4 Tablecloths* at the tea-rooms of St. Pancras Station for the *Northern Adventures* exhibition was a challenge, but great fun. The film *Brief Encounters* seemed to fit that space perfectly.
(1992)

The Critical Decade (this was a publication) marked an important development in the discussion about contemporary black visual art practice over a ten year period.
(1992)

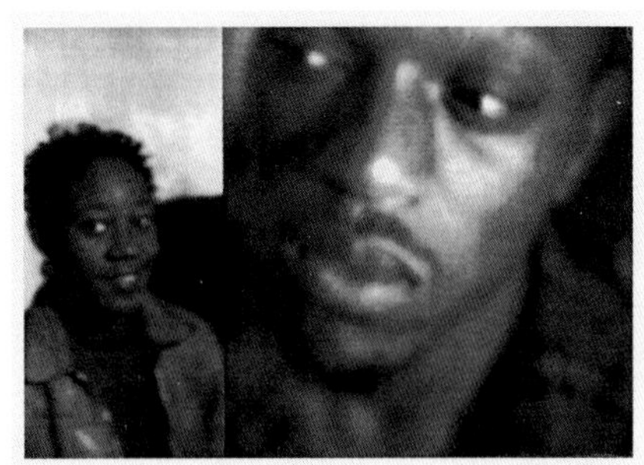

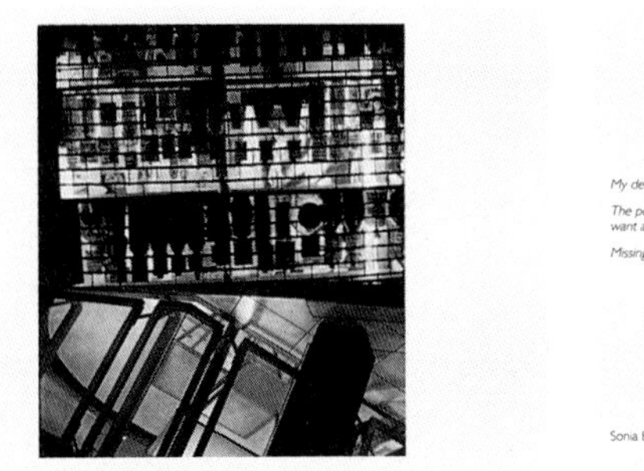

The postcard text (c, Carnival):

My dearest,

It's summer at last and what a scorcher. Everybody's parading and grasping the sun or the warm night air.

Looking quite butch, I masquerade down Colville Terrace on my way to Powis Square. That's when we met. Actually less of a meeting more a moment.

Mesmerised by the dampness shimmering in the parting of his lips. Get up uh ooh baby. Magnetic moments shiver your bone and catch the smile in my eyes.

What a feeling. Everyone's out today. Sliding to the rift of the beat. Amidst the dull bustling humidity. Bump to the rhumba. Pump and bubble down. Don't look now you're being watched and face imminent barricades.

Catch you later.

Sonia Boyce, Carnival, 3 October 1990

c) **Carnival**

The postcard text (d, Late Night Shopping):

My dearest,

The potential to get what I want, when I want, how I want and wherever, remains unfulfilled.

Missing you.

Sonia Boyce, Late Night Shopping, 3 October 1990

d) **Late Night Shopping**

The Ticket Machine 1990
6 postcards

The modern metropolis in Boyce's work is an equivocal and unresolved space which reflects the experiences of its poly-cultural and poly-national inhabitants for whom the city is the repository both of their fears and their desires. The postcards emitted from Boyce's ticket machine speak of the banality of everyday, metropolitan life (bus journeys and management committees), the possibility of sexual adventure (clubbing, carnival) and the points at which these converge in the city ('My dearest,... The potential to get what I want, when I want, how I want and wherever, remains unfulfilled... Missing you,').[5] Boyce's city is neither a modernist utopia nor a postmodern dystopia but rather a place where fragmented experiences and divergent desires are both placed and displaced. The post-colonial metropolis is both here and there, home and away at one and the same time, not unlike the identities of its citizens, which as Stuart Hall has written, are formed:

> ... at the unstable point where the 'unspeakable' stories of subjectivity meet the narratives of a history, of a culture. And since he/she is positioned in relation to cultured narratives which have been profoundly expropriated the colonised subject is always 'somewhere else': doubly marginalized, displaced always other than where he or she is, or is able to speak from.[6]

Exposing the presence of individual narratives which weave their way through the anonymous fabric of the city, Boyce's installation pieces for *The Invisible City* belong to a 'series' of other works made over a five-year period between 1988 and 1993, which explore the intersection of private life and public spectacle within the city. In the British Art Show of 1990, Boyce exhibited *Colour photograph* (1989), a self-portrait printed on colour photocopy in which the artist frames her face with her hands, drawing the viewer's eyes to a dark, rectangular patch overlaying the right-hand corner of her face and accentuating the texture and colour of her red lips which seem almost in relief. While the image hung in the exhibition amongst the other works selected for the show, Boyce wrote an accompanying text which she placed in the dating magazine *Contact* alongside the 'lonely hearts' advertisements, inserting her own narrative of desire into the 'real' narratives already in circulation in the city:

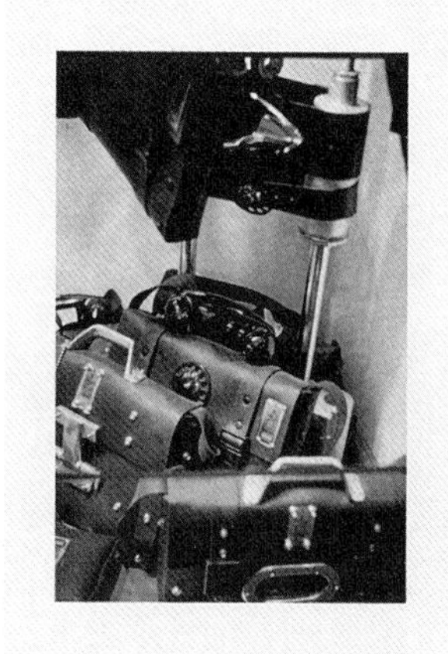

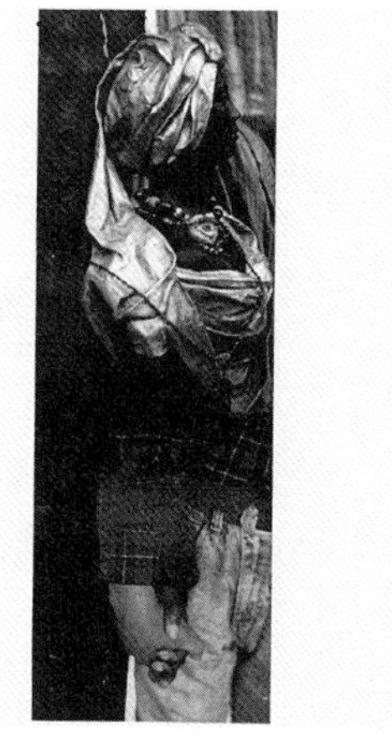

The reproduced postcard (e) reads:

My dearest,

The wait at the bus stop can take a while. Twenty minutes maybe. Ask the conductor to put you off at the petrol station. The house is directly opposite. Try to get there for 8pm.

When you get there the conversation will be warm and familiar. Someone will clear their throat. Then the business will begin.

The agenda is drawn and quartered: funding bodies; rotating chair; NALGO reps; paper sales; anti-everything demos; mortgage repayments; notification from the bank (pause for laughter); the bailiffs; special items; no smoking; fitness plans; workaholics anonymous; relationships versus celibacy; hidden agendas; devisive strategies; any other business; digestives and tea all round.

Mary and Ann-Marie will slip away half way through the evening. They always do. The rest of us will shift and curl up on the bed, sofa and floor.

In the morning we'll wake up with Kiss FM, back aches, sore throats and stiff necks.

In sisterhood,

Sonia Boyce, Management Committee, 3 October 1990

London Project II: The Invisible City, The Photographers' Gallery, London, 19 October – 1 December 1990

e) **Management Committee**

The reproduced postcard (f) reads:

My dearest,

Let me take you there. Let me melt you chocolate hard, up against the fridge. Rewind. Rewind. Rewind me slow. Dirty nasty love. Mix me down operator. Thick thighs swirl between her. Venus rising. My word what two fingers can do. Scratch mix and pull up in the cold night air, waiting for the early morning bus home.

Lots of love,

Sonia Boyce, Clubbing, 3 October 1990

London Project II: The Invisible City, The Photographers' Gallery, London, 19 October – 1 December 1990

f) **Clubbing**

The Ticket Machine 1990
6 postcards

He blushed each time they met in public.
    Tigger seeks Winnie the Pooh
    to share pots of honey
    and lots of bouncing
All she wanted to know…
Was it good for you to know she knew you.
Her eyes sparkled each time they met in public.
    Well heeled wild angel
    seeks
    creamy velvet underground
    for funky business
As she caressed her hand in hand, she wondered,
would anyone know?[7]

Shortly afterwards, Boyce made *Pillowcase* (1990), a seven-foot pillowcase on which the artist imprinted lonely hearts ads on a massive scale. For the first time, Boyce used real advertisements, culled from the lonely hearts pages which elicited an uncomfortable response from viewers who felt uneasy standing in front of this vast re-construction of advertisements which are usually read surreptitiously, as an illicit and intimate activity. The appeal for Boyce of the small ads lay in their status as 'fragments of life', partial narratives which like art works are fabricated by their authors according to predetermined rules and formats. With *Pillowcase*, Boyce quite literally exposed personal desire to public gaze and transformed traces of private intimacy into a spectacle for public scrutiny. Created as a sculptural work, the physical shape of the piece itself played on the notion of inner and outer as mutually exclusive categories. As with the earlier work *Talking Presence*, Boyce confounds the traditional dichotomy between an inside and an outside space and hence the relationships between the macro-structures of the city (for example, public spaces, social, cultural and historical narratives and so on) and the micro-structures (domestic spaces, personal histories and individual narratives). In other words, for Boyce the configurations of the metropolitan body are inseparable from those of the individual human body negotiating the city's inner and outer spaces. Nowhere is this more evident than in the work *The Beginning Of An Urban Survival Kit* which Boyce made for the exhibition *Portable Fabric Shelters*, organised by the London Printworks Trust in Brixton in April 1995. Using an ordinary

I'd been playing with old bits of my hair, and shop bought pieces of hair for a while. Maybe it's because I was feeling removed from the tactile engagement with materials. Anyway this 'playing' culminated in an installation called *Do You Want To Touch?* (1993)

Began to think about 'Primitivism' and 'Fetishism'. (1993)

dome-shaped plastic tent as a frame, Boyce imprinted her own photographic images of a human face onto the fabric of the tent. The portable tent designed to shelter the human body from the ravages of wind and rain (and, we could infer, equally from the social and economic hardships of the modern city) is itself fabricated from the fragments of an individual human body which functions both as sign and object, as part and whole at the same time. Not only is this a metaphor for our relationship to the post-colonial metropolis but potentially also for our relationship to the work of art which creates a space into which the viewer can enter as if, as the artist says, 'you were getting into someone's head'.[8]

In many ways, 1990 was a crucial year for Sonia Boyce. As I have argued elsewhere, this particular year was both a formal and conceptual watershed in the work not only of Boyce but of several of her peers.[9] With *Pillowcase*, Boyce evacuated from her work for the first time the figurative bodies which had dominated her large-scale drawings in the 1980s and the absent presence of a literal body haunts her work for the next five years. Even in works such as *This One's Dedicated To Everybody Who Knows Me* (1991), where recognisable faces appear within the frame of the work, they do so as a partial presence, laughing heads 'plugged' into the complex circuitry of an electronic grid which has usurped their physical bodies. At the same time that the narrative pictorial genre was displaced in Boyce's work, so language and text began to play a less prominent role in works made after 1990 (with the notable exception of *4 Tablecloths*). Conversely, the role of audience became increasingly important in the artist's work as Boyce sought to create a space between the work and the audience into which the viewer could enter. Boyce's works increasingly relied on the audience's interaction with them and the viewer's gaze as a vital ingredient of their artistic intention. The role of the viewer in Boyce's installations from *Do You Want To Touch?* (Central 181 Gallery, 1993), *Wish You Were Here* (Bank, 1994) and *peep* (Brighton Museum and Art Gallery, 1995), discussed at length above, culminated in two works in the latter half of 1995, Boyce's *Untitled (Kiss)* installation (commissioned by the Institute of International Visual Arts for the Mirage exhibition at the Institute of Contemporary Arts in May 1995) and her large-scale installation '... *they're almost like twins*' for the exhibition *Cottage Industry* at Beaconsfield and associated sites in November of that year.

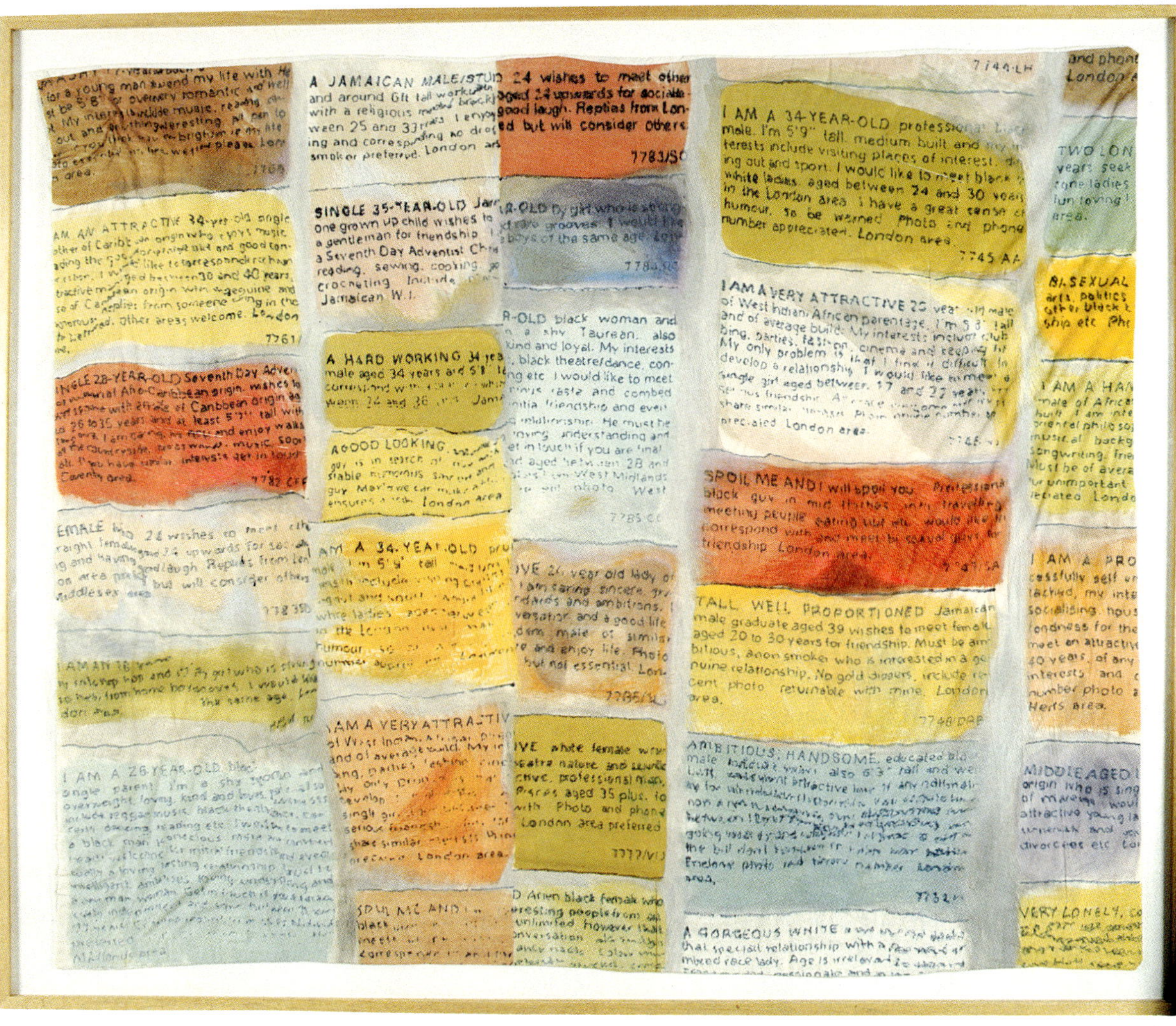

Pillowcase 1990
mixed media on cotton

The work of Frantz Fanon and, in particular *Black Skin, White Masks,* published in 1958, provided the focus for a season of events at the ICA in the summer of 1995, curated by David A. Bailey, which included an exhibition of works by eight artists from the UK, USA and Martinique. Boyce created a new work for the exhibition: a massive colour print of a mixed race couple (a black woman and a white man) which she installed in a narrow space, wedged between the two large spaces making up the upper galleries; on the opposite wall, facing the image of the couple on the point of kissing, Boyce hung two small images – one of an all-white audience clapping and the other of a black audience. The artist's positioning of the two elements of the work forces the viewer into the space between the kissing couple and their applauding audiences, creating what David Bailey has described as an 'arena for the spectacle of miscegenation' in which the viewer is compelled to look upon this intimate and conventionally taboo union at uncomfortably close quarters or, alternatively, to view at an awkward distance their 'mirror image': two audiences celebrating the segregation of the races.[10] Boyce's work articulates a critique of Fanon's uncompromising disdain for the 'woman of colour' who forms a sexual relationship with a white man whom he caricatures through the real-life figure of Mayotte Capécia in *Black Skin, White Masks.*[11] At the same time, the artist points to the aversion and censure which such mixed race relationships elicit among black and white communities alike. The spectacle of inter-racial desire which Boyce stages for public view not only transgresses the discrete domains of private and public life, but defies the avowed impossibility of inter-racial relationships to assert 'the possibility of mutual desire':

The Audiences

The Guardians of the gate: the judgement
How could you (choose)?

Beneath the silent gaze, each says:
**what does he see in her, doesn't he
recognise what she (symbolically)
represents**

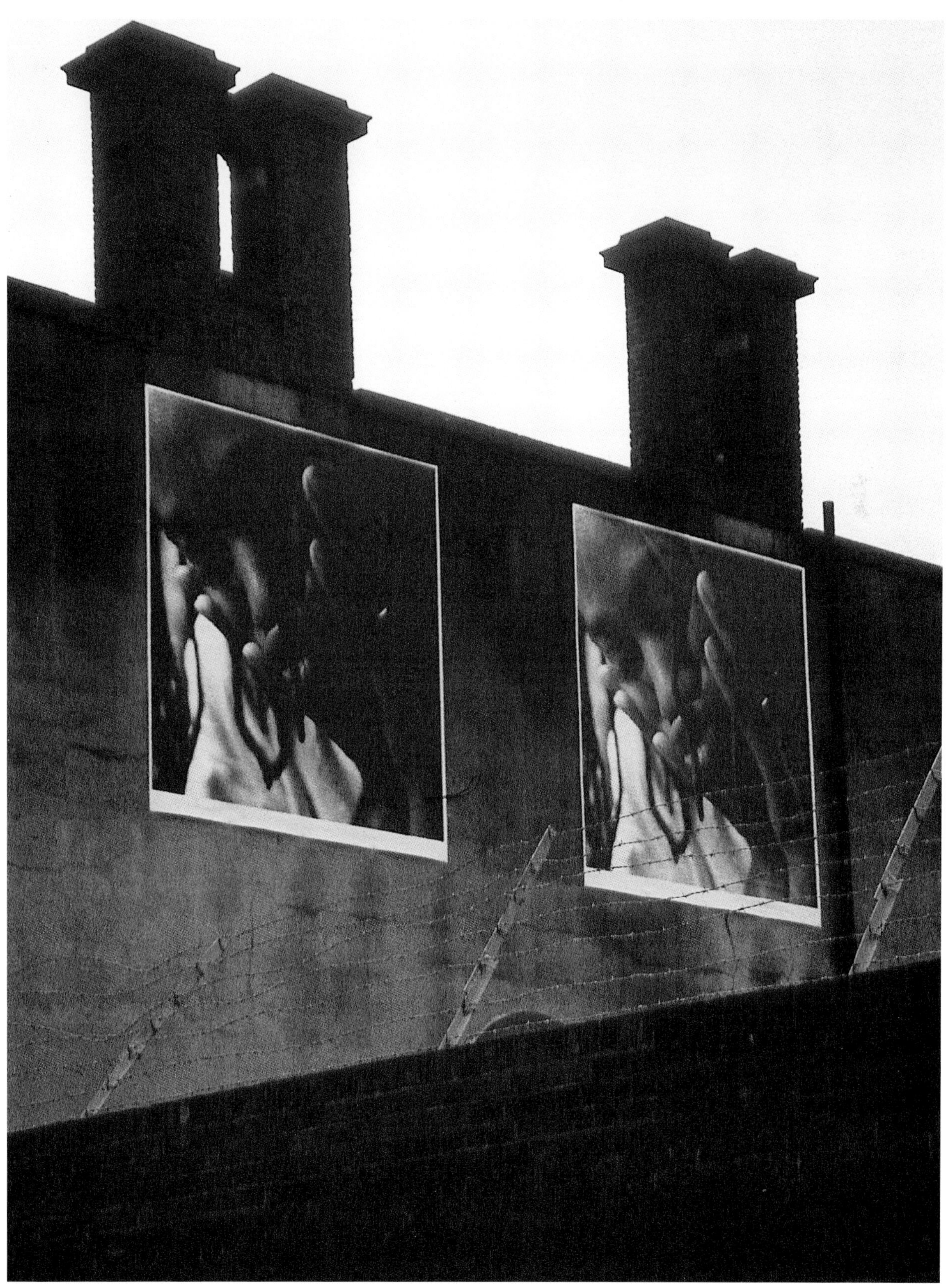

installation view of **They're Almost Like Twins** 1995

Overleaf: **Untitled (Kiss)** 1995
ink jet print onto heavy duty vinyl

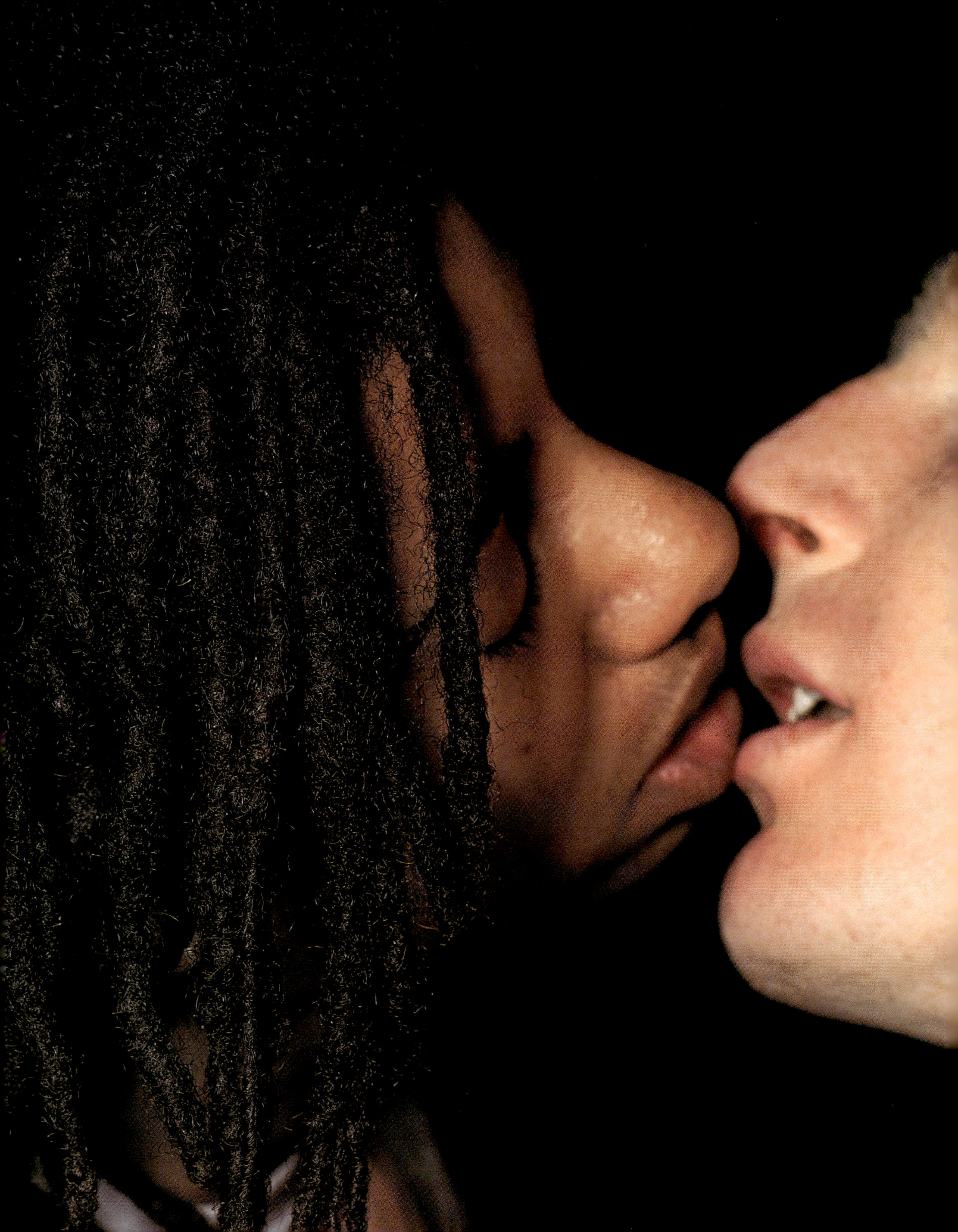

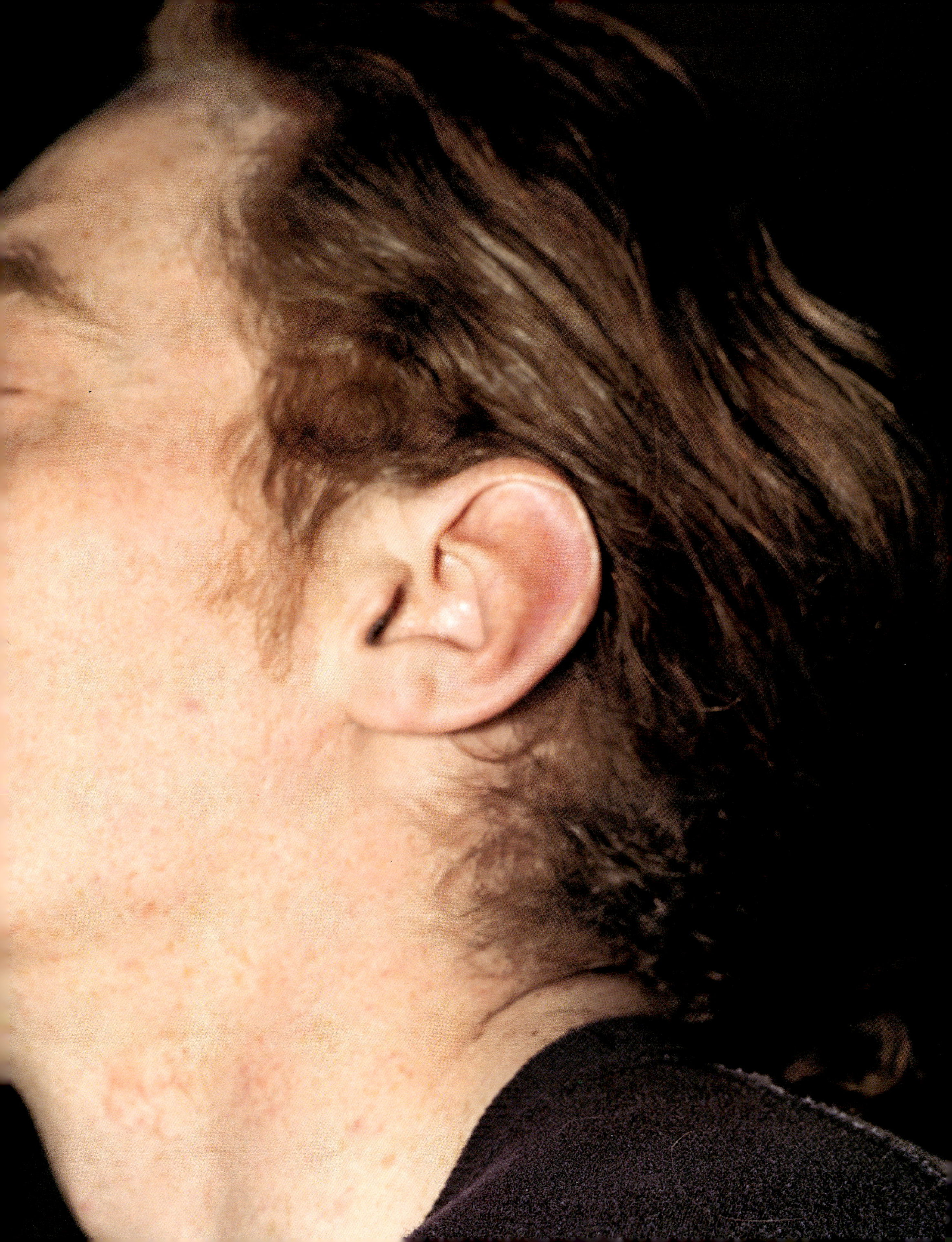

what does she see in him, doesn't she recognise what he (symbolically) represents.

Each side believing that this desire signals a refusal, that it abandons them.
Whenever, in the public domain, the question of the relationship between black and white is discussed (normally the black male and the white female), we have to begin with denial. We have to begin with the idea that such a relationship is ultimately doomed. That one identity will have to subsume the other. We have to distance ourselves from the possibility of mutual desire.[12]

At Beaconsfield, on an external rendered wall facing the railway track which winds its way around the back of Beaconsfield's nineteenth century building, Boyce mounted two vast black and white photographic portraits. Reminiscent of *Colour photograph* from the British Art Show, the figure cradles her tilting face between her hands, filling the full expanse of the image. Installed like billboard posters below two matching chimneys without any frame or accompanying text, the images appear identical at first glance, echoing the architectural features of the building. Designed to be glimpsed within a fraction of a minute from a moving train, these works disrupt the familiar conventions of the advertising hoardings which tend to conform to the rule of communicating a clear, repeatable and legible message. By contrast, Boyce's *They're Almost Like Twins* is contradictory: the images are not identical (one being markedly darker than the other); they appear to be intimate, personal photographs, enlarged and relocated to a public site without any obvious reason; and, rather than becoming clearer through repetition, their 'message' is rendered more enigmatic. Being the same but different simultaneously, these two images make visible within the public domain the moment of recognition and disavowal of racial difference which Fanon describes so vividly in *Black Skin, White Masks* and which is enacted not in the colonial city but rather in the European metropolis, the capital of what Fanon calls 'the mother country':

'Mama, see the Negro! I'm frightened! Frightened! Frightened! … I could no longer laugh, because I already knew that there

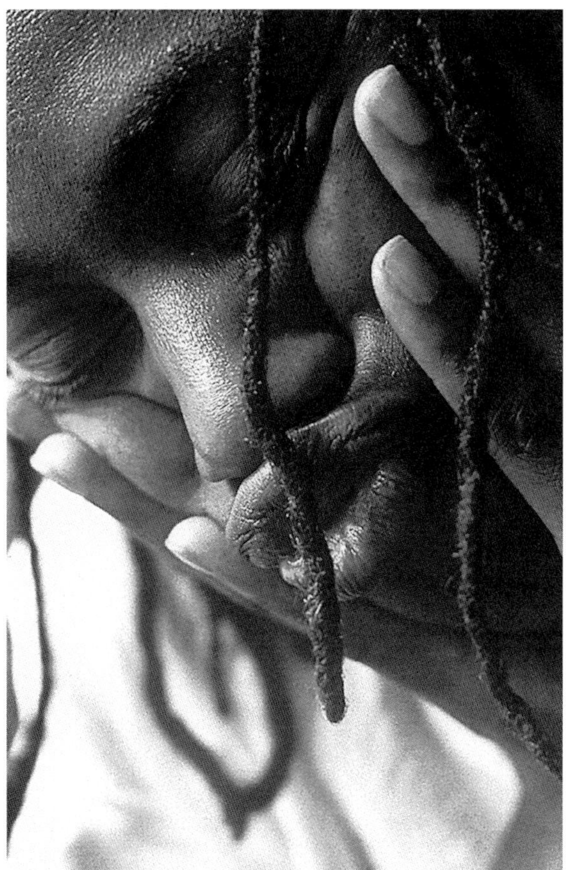 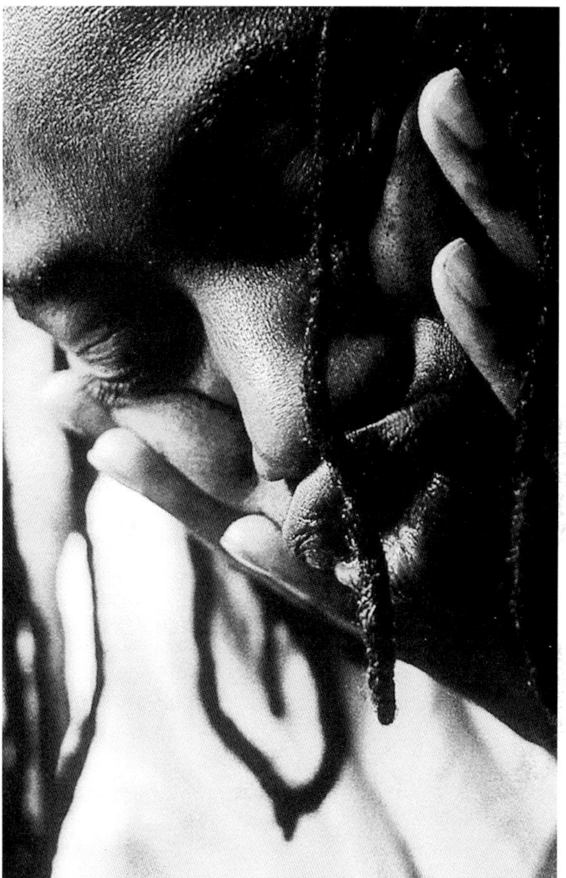

They're Almost Like Twins 1995
ink jet prints onto heavy duty vinyl

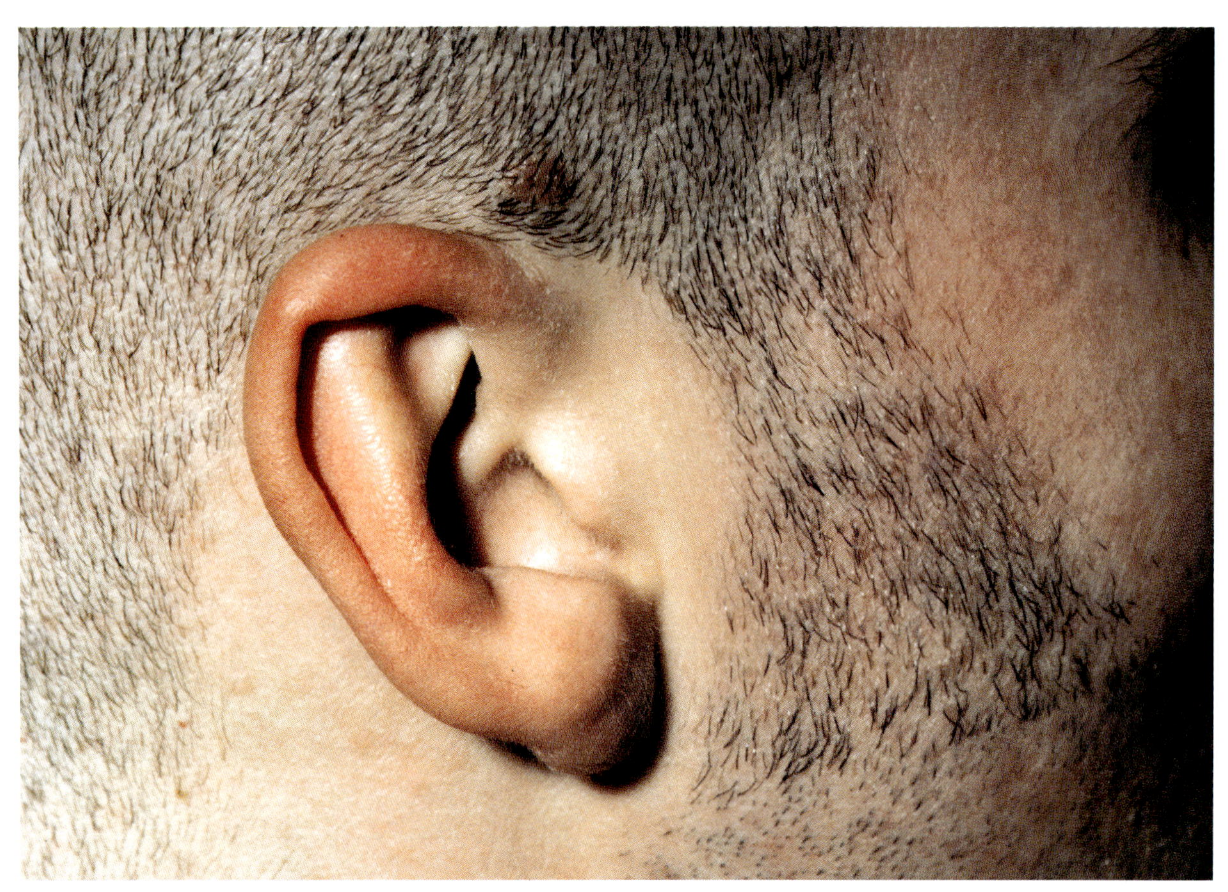

Head I (Skin) 1995
photo silk screen street posters

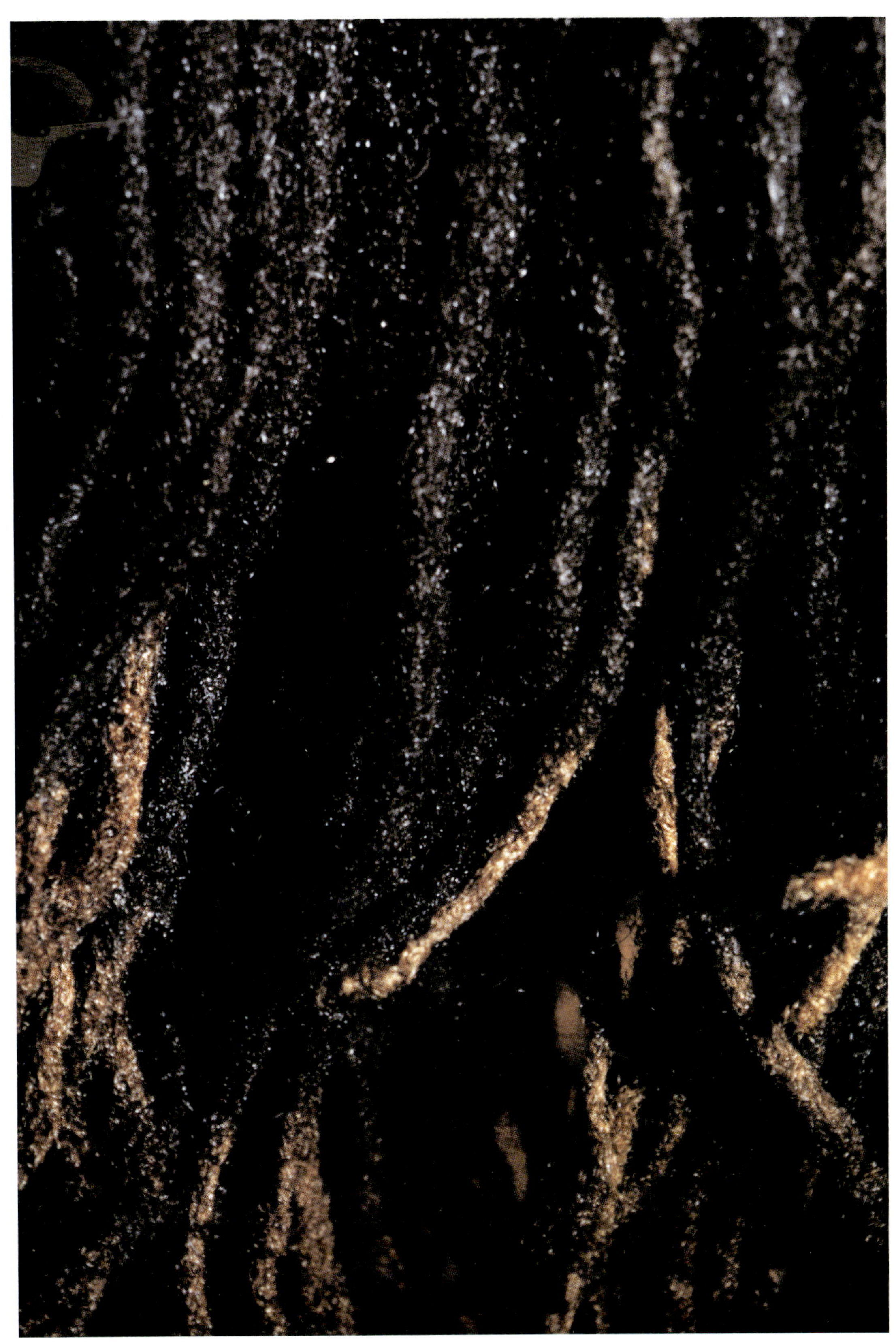

Head II (Dread) 1995
photo silk screen street posters

were legends, stories, history, and above all *historicity*... Then at various points the corporeal schema crumbled, its place taken by a racial epidermal schema. In the train it was no longer a question of being aware of my body in the third person but in a triple person. In the train, I was given not one but two, three places... I existed triply: I occupied space. I moved toward the other... and the evanescent other, hostile but not opaque, transparent, not there, disappeared... I was responsible at the same time for my body, for my race for my ancestors. I subjected myself to an objective examination, I discovered my blackness. [13]

In response to Boyce's installation, the viewer's fleeting gaze from the train is caught in a literal 'double-take' which at first disavows and then recognises the difference between the two images and displaces the corporeal schema for the 'racial epidermal schema'. In other words, the single, repeated image of a woman becomes split into the images of two (almost identical) women, one dark-skinned, the other light-skinned. In that split second of recognition and disavowal, the viewer's gaze fixes its subject with the fact of her blackness. As the train moves away, across the bridge which links the south of the city to Europe, Boyce's images remain fixed to the rendered wall of the nineteenth century building, mute witnesses to the narratives of fear and desire which permeate the fabric of the post-colonial metropolis.

1   Italo Calvino, *Invisible Cities*, 1976, p.36.

2   'Underground' by Sonia Boyce (1990), first published
    in *Distinguishing Marks*, exhibition catalogue, Panchayat,
    London, 1990.

3   Sonia Boyce from 'Proposal for 4 Tablecloths', unpublished.

4   David Chandler, 'Introduction', *The Invisible City*, exhibition
    catalogue, The Photographers' Gallery, London, 1990.

5   Sonia Boyce, 'Late Night Shopping, 3 October 1990',
    The Invisible City, The Photographers' Gallery, London,
    1990.

6   Stuart Hall, 'Minimal Selves', *Identity: The Real Me*,
    ICA Documents 6, London, Institute of Contemporary Arts,
    1987, p.44.

7   Sonia Boyce, text from her project for *The British Art
    Show*, South Bank Centre, 1990. Boyce has continued to
    revise this lonely hearts text the original version read:

    He blushed each time they met in public.
        Tigger seeks Winnie the Pooh
        to share pots of honey
        and bouncing
    All she wanted to know
    Was it good for you?
    Was it good for you? Too. Know she knew you.
    Her eyes sparkled each time they met in public.
        Well heeled wild angel
        seeks
        creamy velvet underground
    As she caressed. Her hand in hand. She wondered.
    Would anyone know?

8   Sonia Boyce from *Portable Fabric Shelters*, exhibition
    catalogue, London, London Printworks Trust, 1995.

9   See my essay, 'The Sphinx Contemplating Napoleon'
    in Katy Deepwell (ed.) *New Feminist Art Criticism*,
    Manchester, Manchester University Press, 1995.

10 David A. Bailey, 'Enigmas of Race, Difference and Desire',
    from *Mirage: Enigmas of Race, Difference and Desire*,
    exhibition catalogue, London, Institute of Contemporary
    Arts and Institute of International Visual Arts, London,
    1995, p.70.

11 See Frantz Fanon, 'The Woman of Color and the White
    Man', in *Black Skin, White Masks*, Pluto Press, London,
    1986, pp.41–62.

12 Sonia Boyce from proposal for *Mirage* project (unpublished).

13 Frantz Fanon, *Black Skin, White Masks*, Pluto Press,
    London, 1986, p.112.

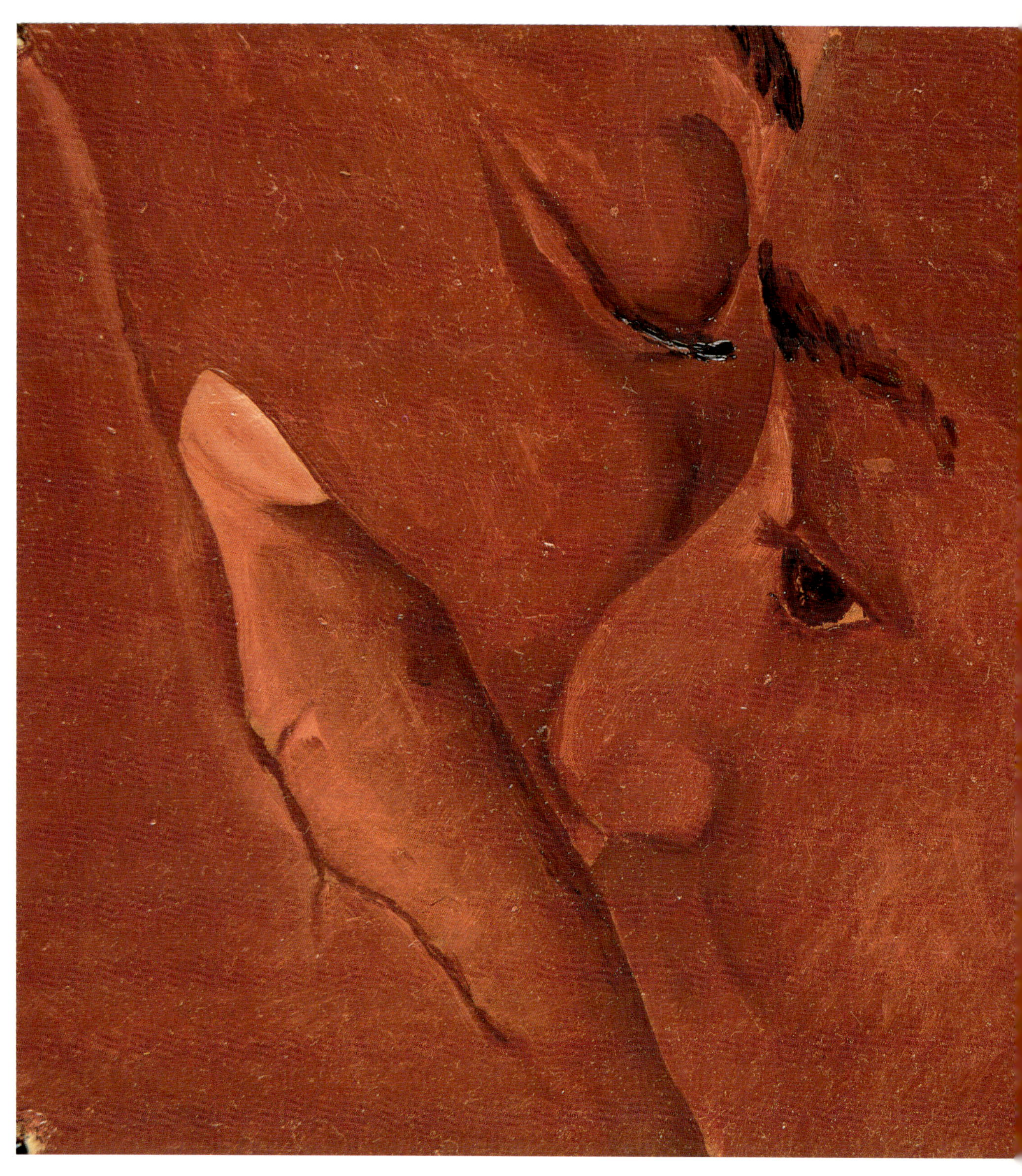

Kiss 1992
oil on paper

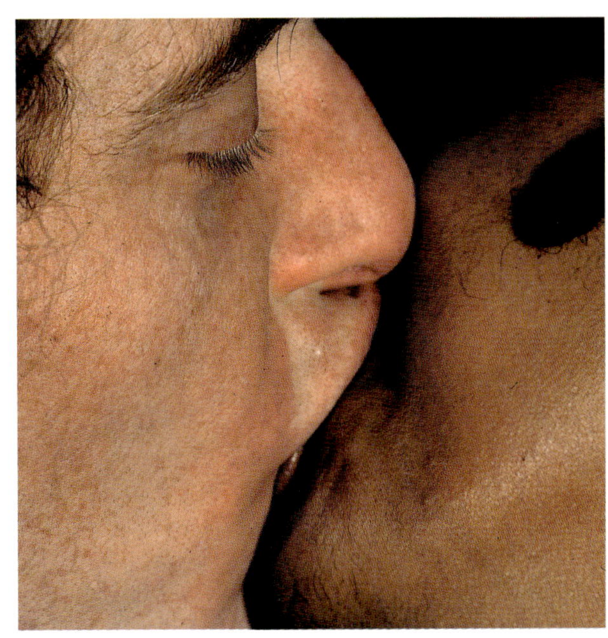

Mm... 1995
colour photograph

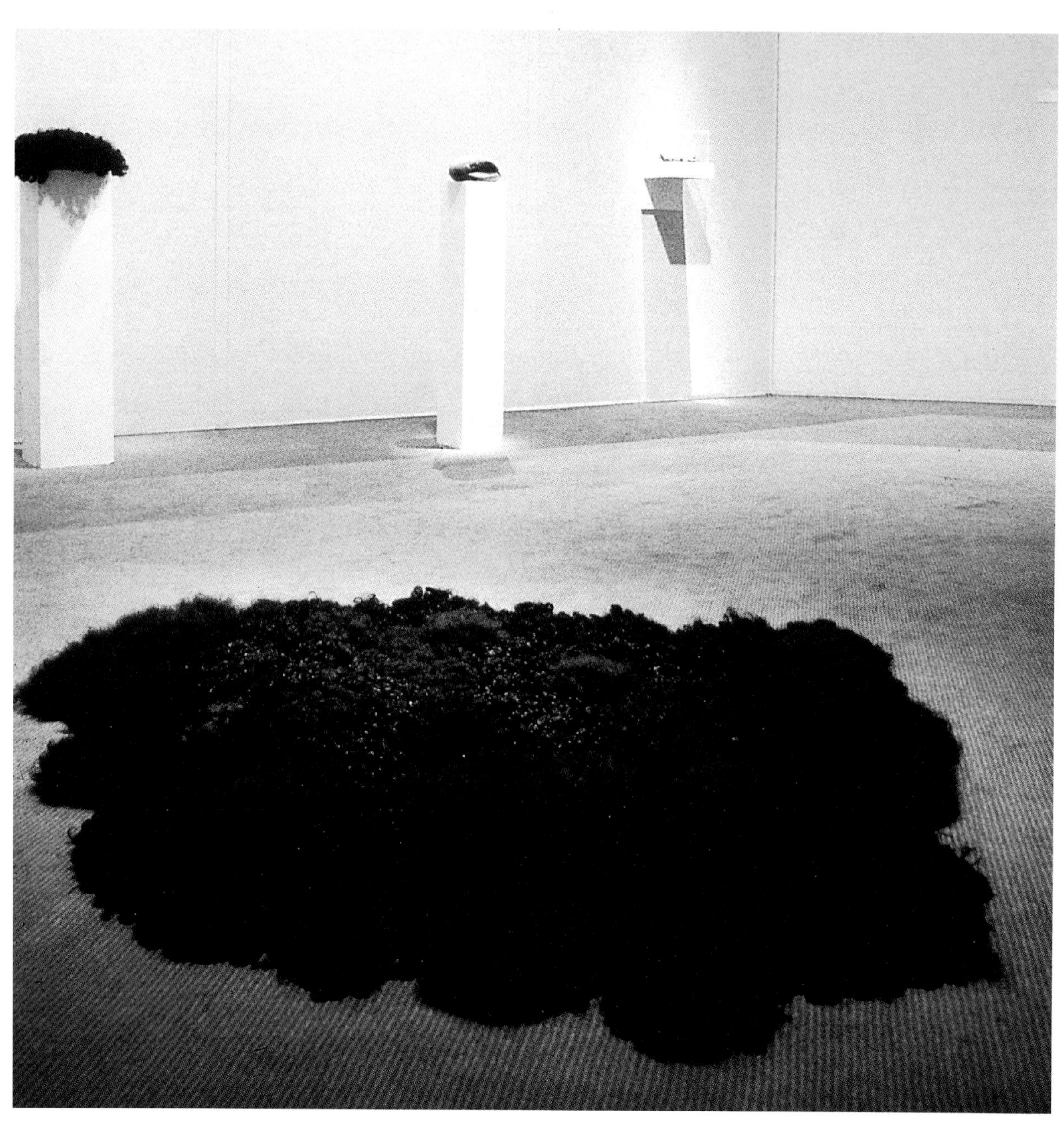

installation view of **Afro Blanket** 1994
37 afro wigs

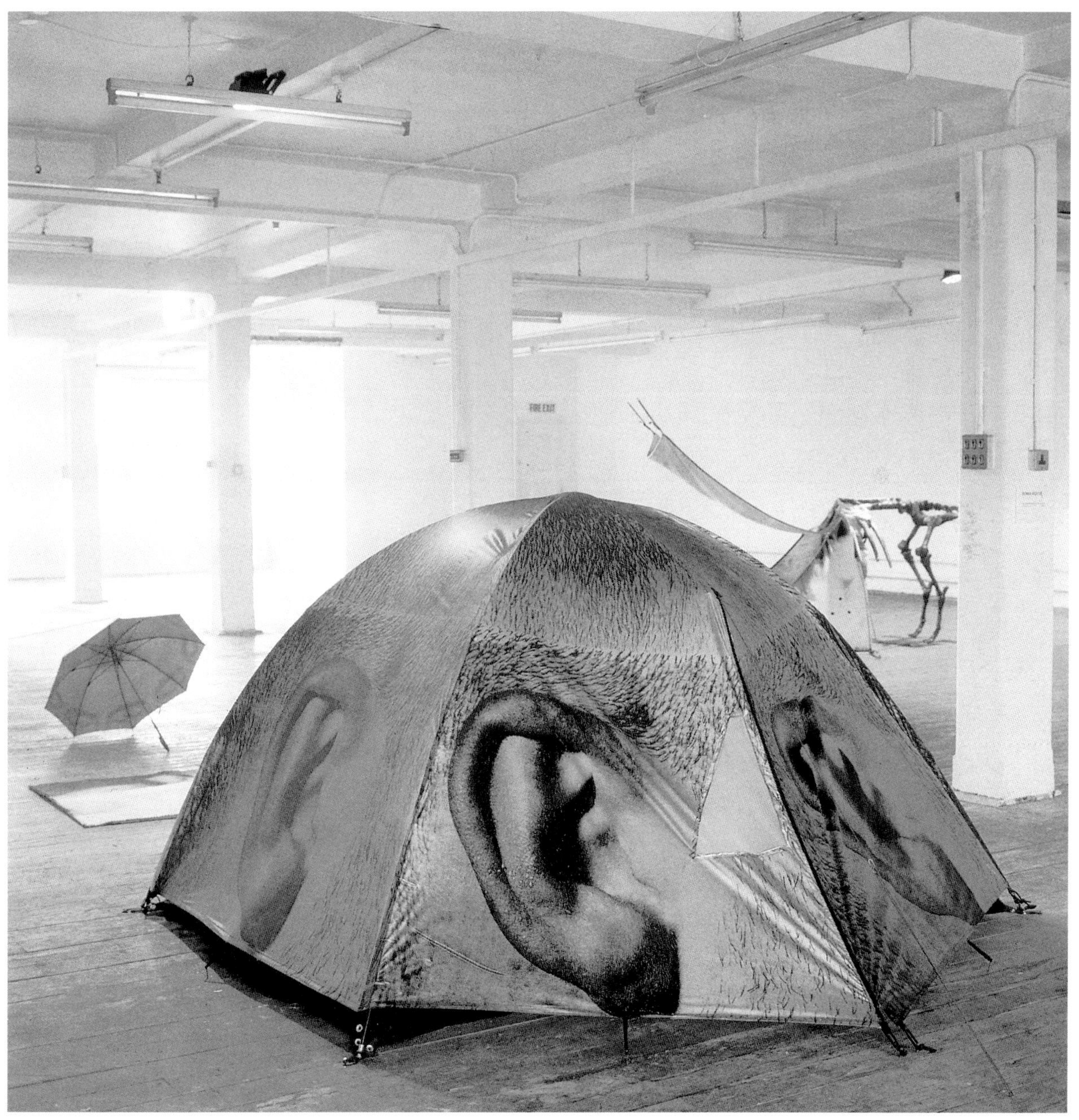

installation view of **Tent** 1995
photo silk screen print on tent

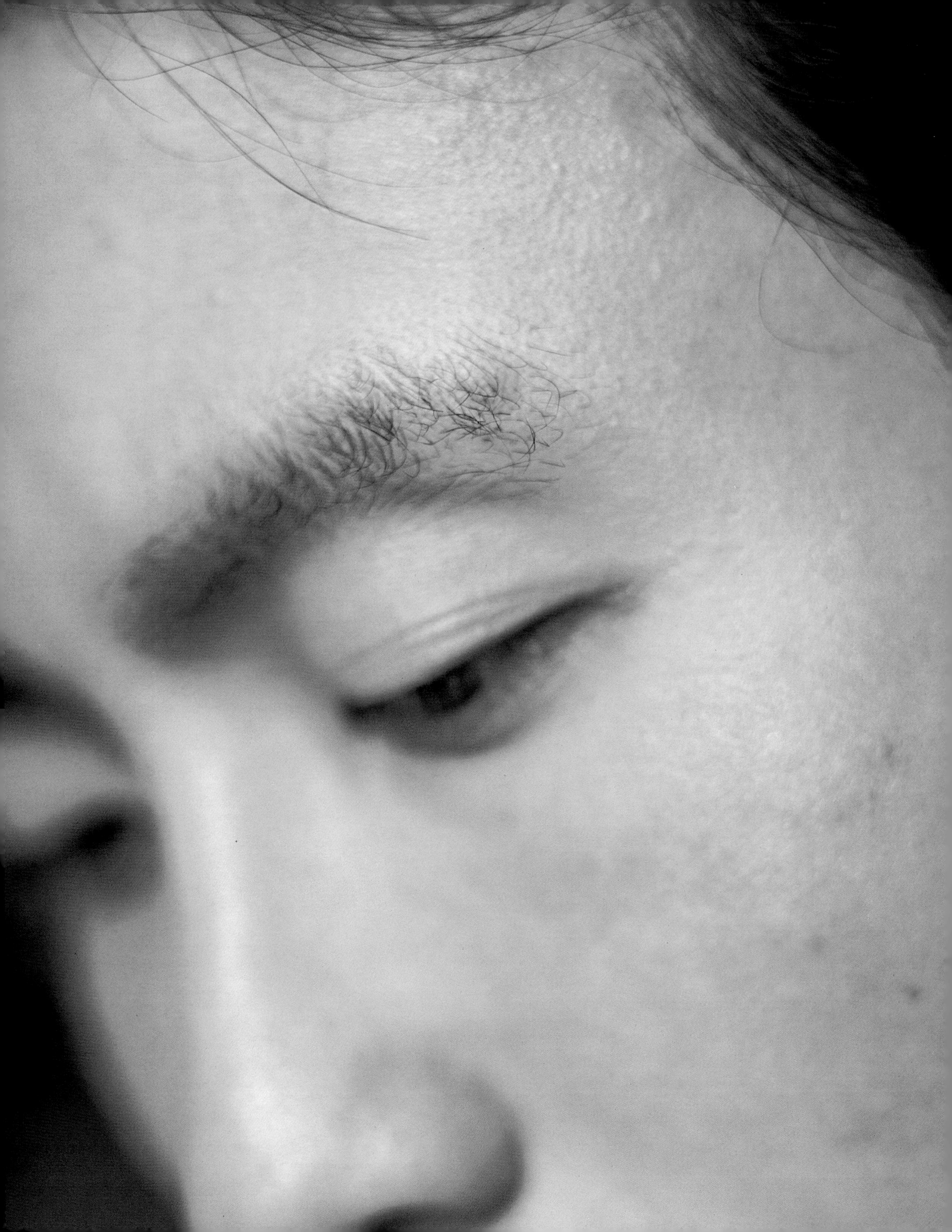

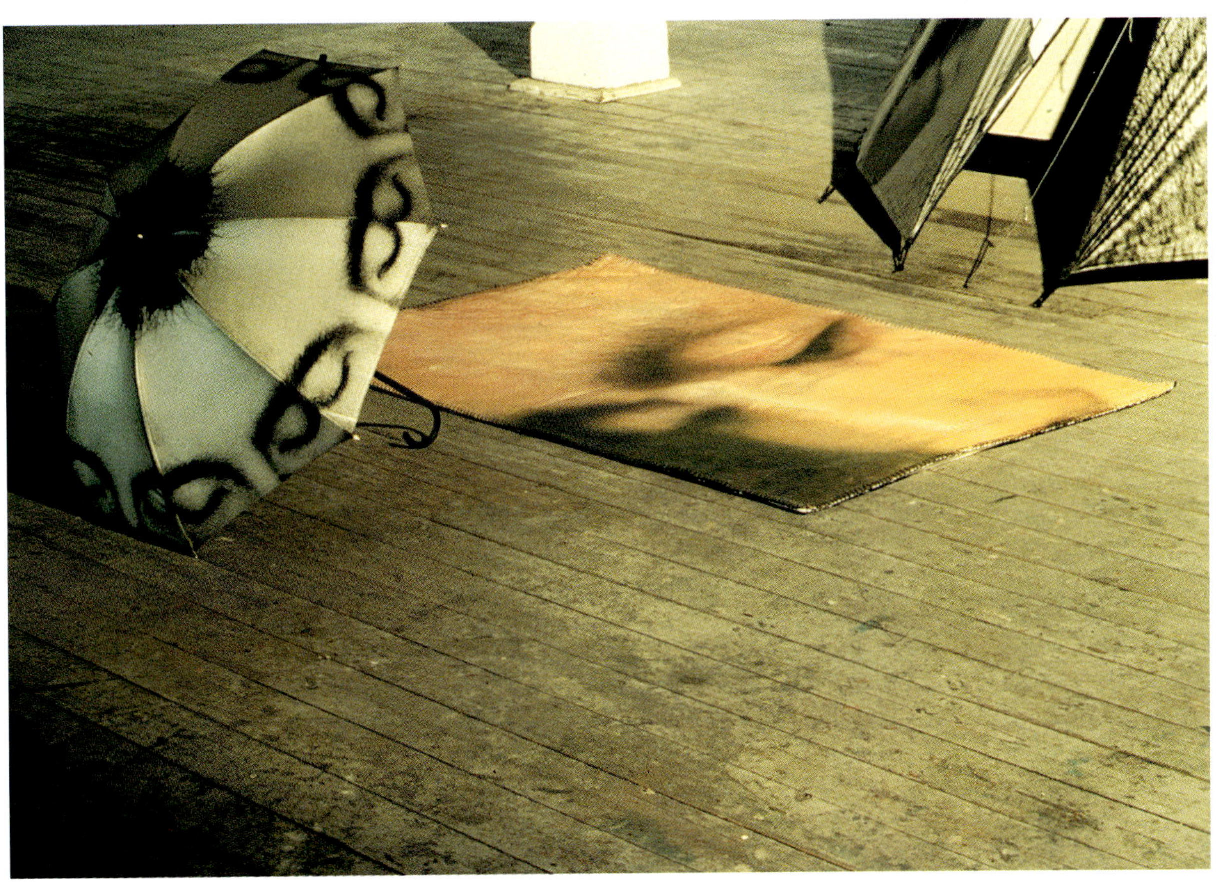

installation view of **Tent, Blanket and Umbrella –
The Beginnings Of An Urban Survival Kit** 1995

Blanket 1995
photo silk screen print on cotton

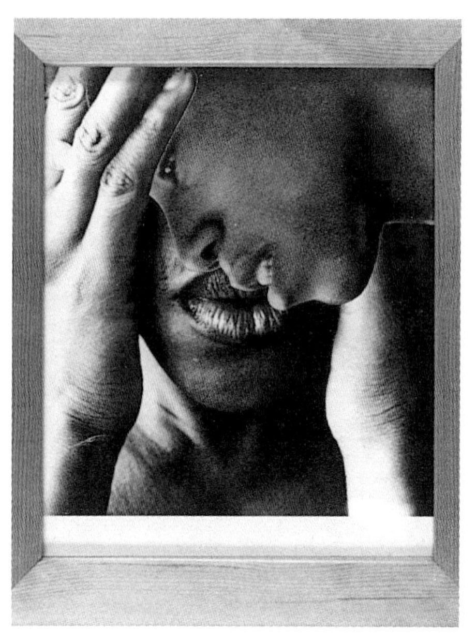

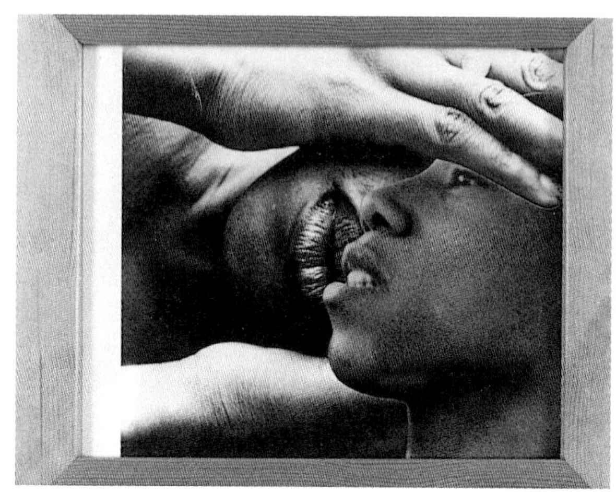

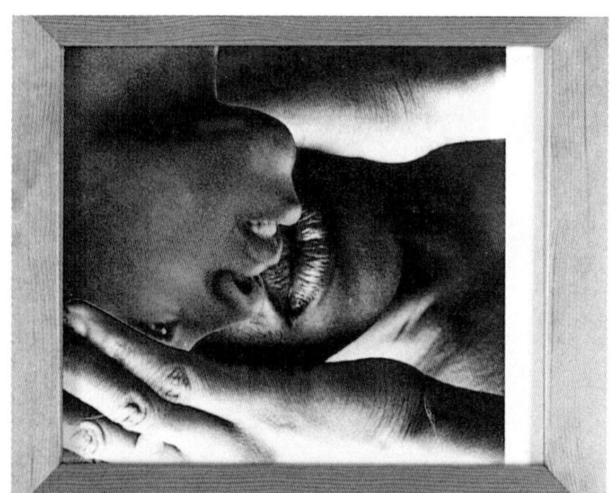

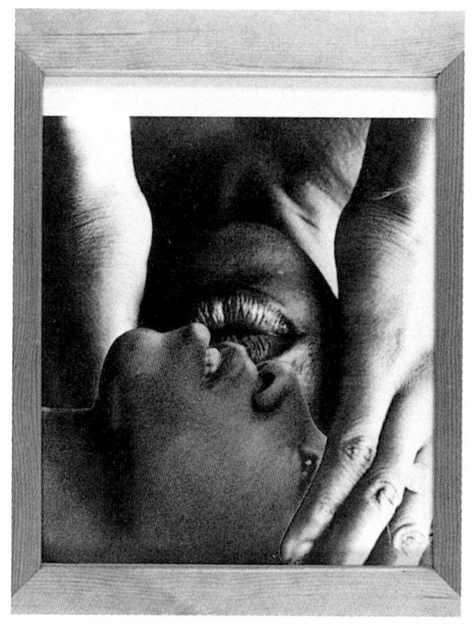

Love In A Cold Climate 1988
collage

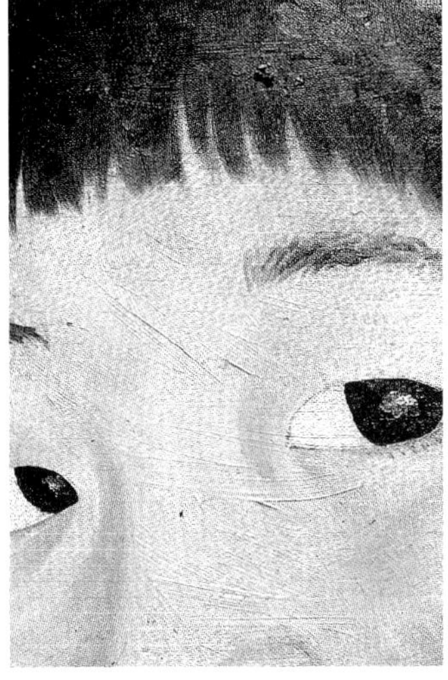 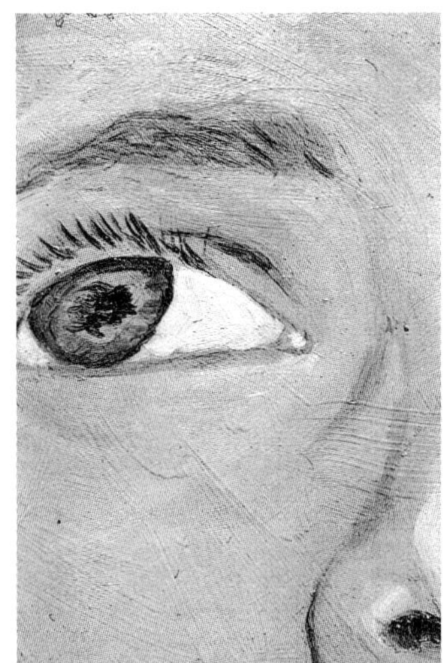 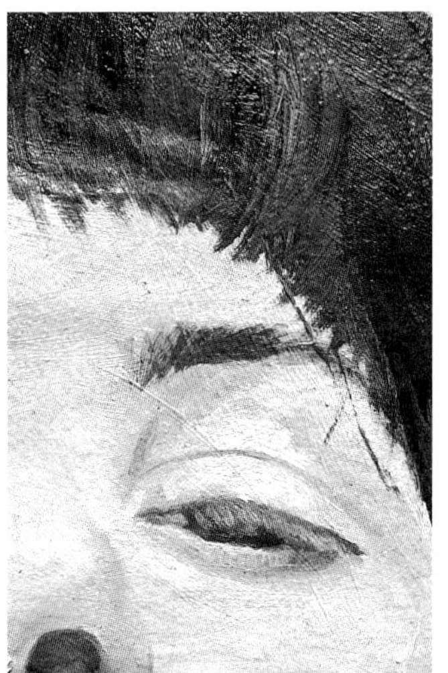

a) **Fragment** sketch 1992   oil on paper
b) **Fragment** sketch 1992   oil on paper
c) **Fragment** sketch 1992   oil on paper

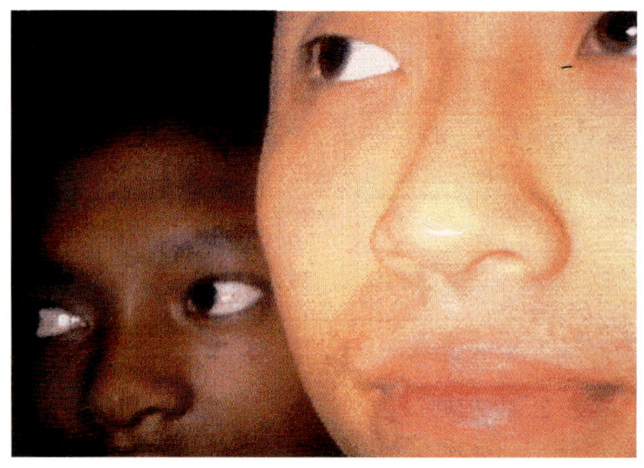

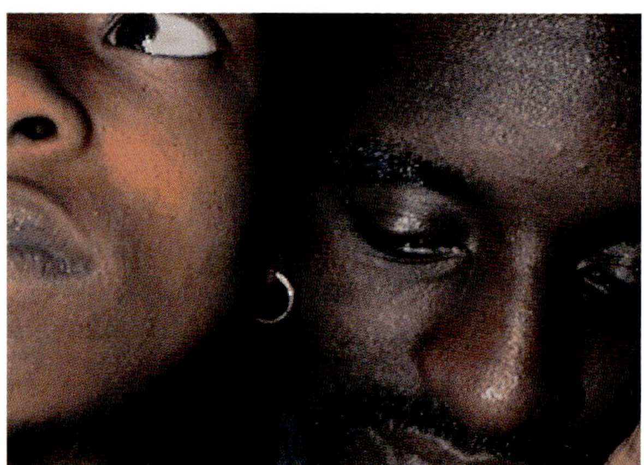

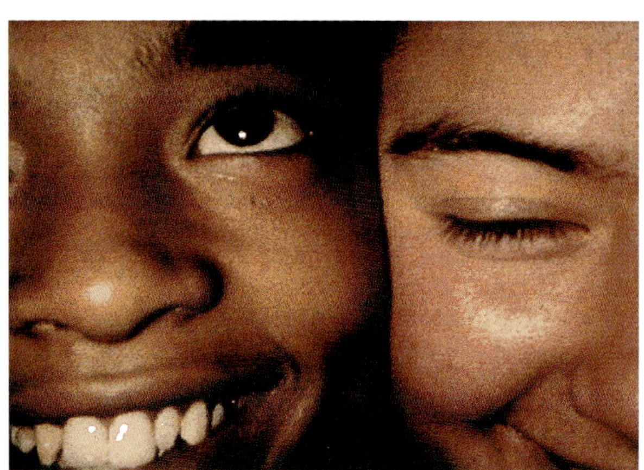

digital stills from the **Too Close For Comfort** 1991
video

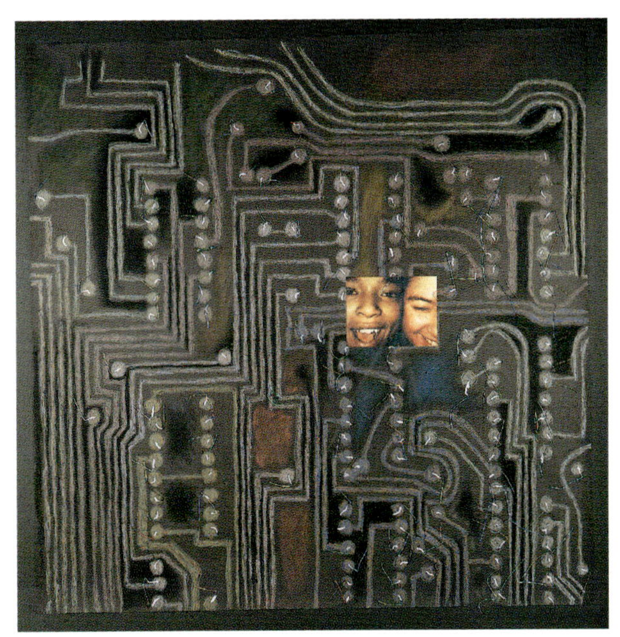

This One's Dedicated To Everybody Who Knows Me 1991
pastels and laser copy on paper

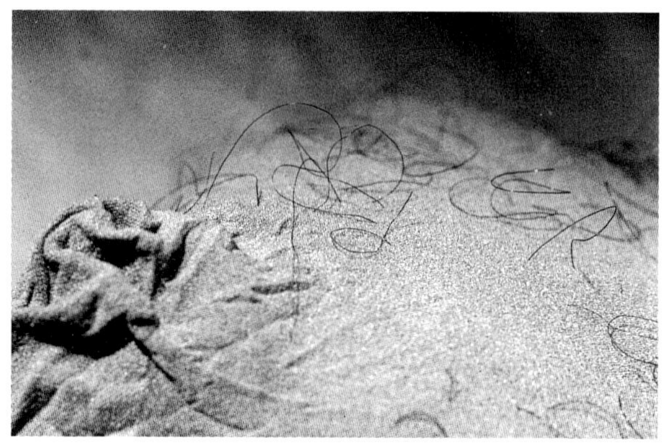

Three Legs Of Tights Stuffed With Hair 1995
colour photographs

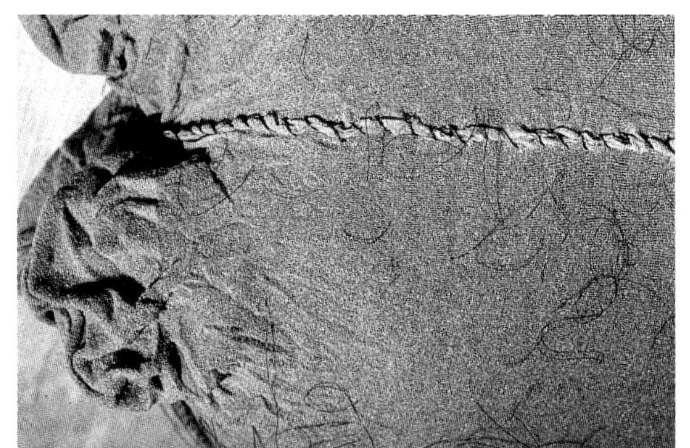 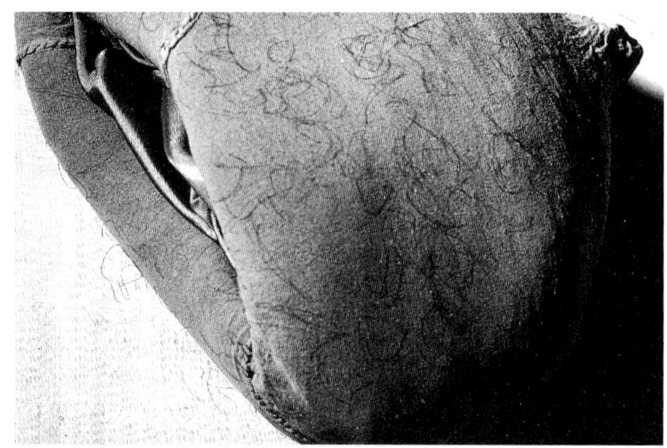

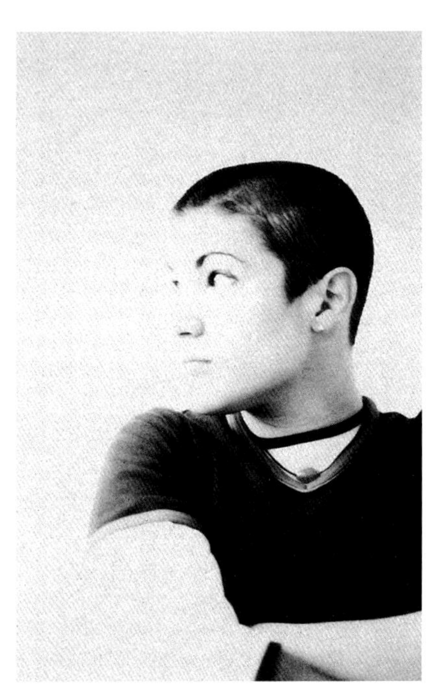

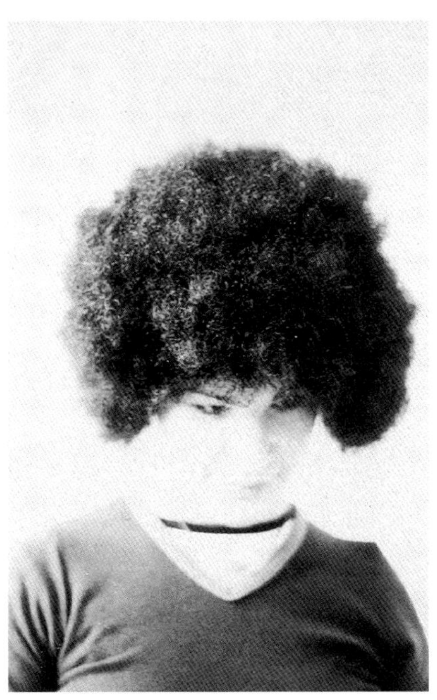

Claire and Afro 1996
black and white photographs

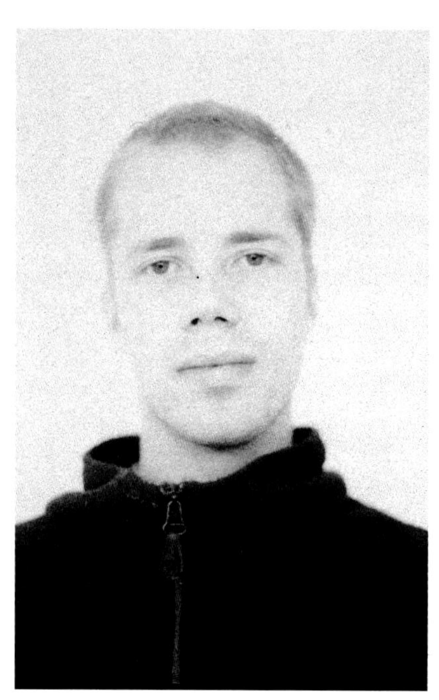

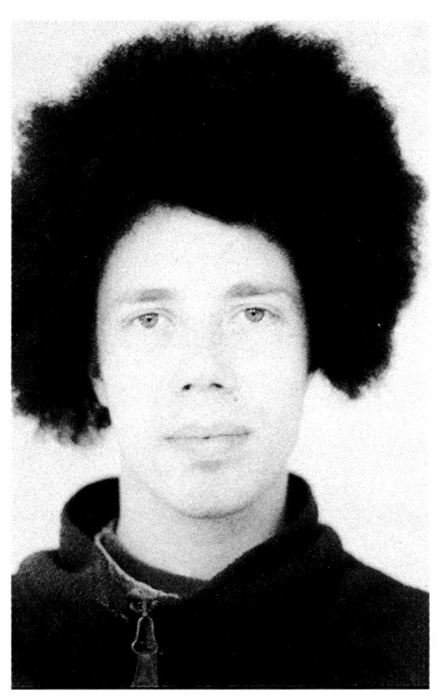

Stuart and Afro 1996
black and white photographs

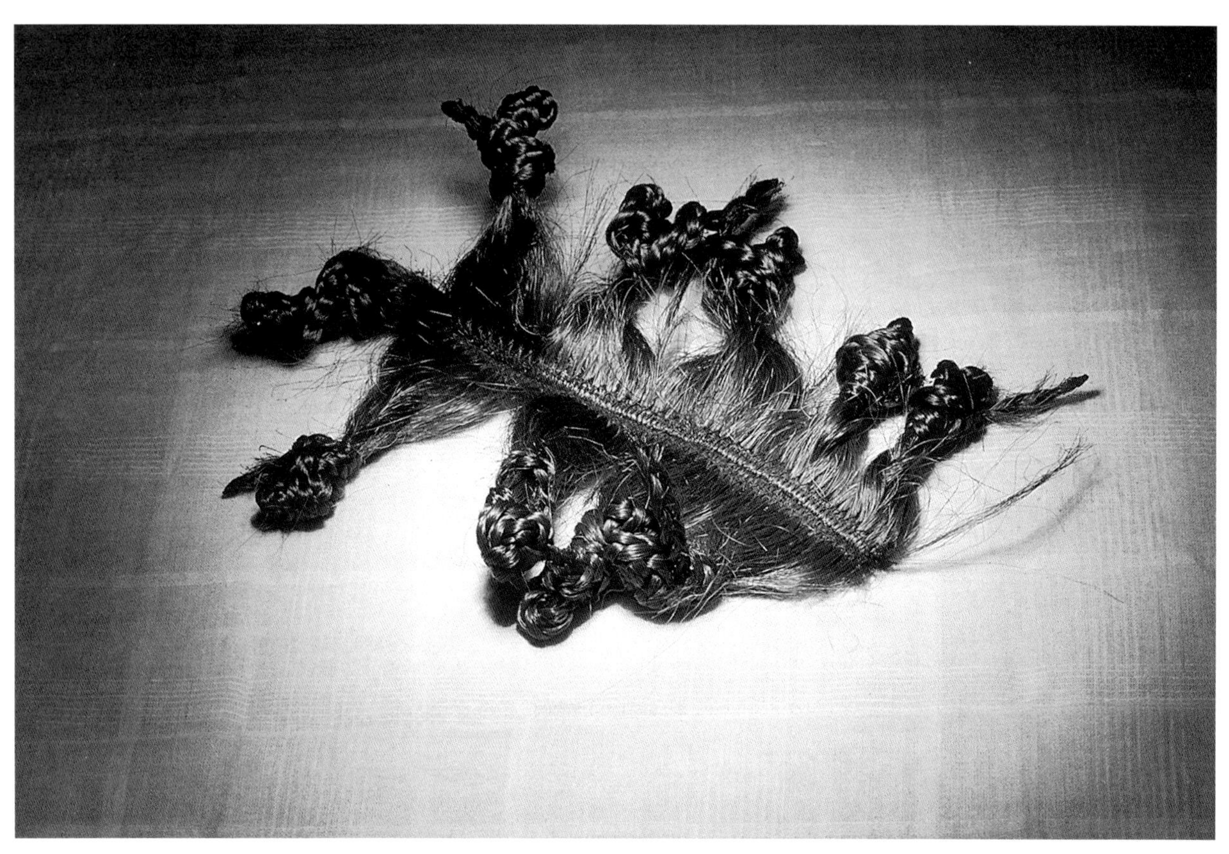

Plaited And Knotted 1995
colour photograph

Sonia Boyce

Sonia Boyce was born in Islington, London, in 1962. After
studying for a year at East Ham College of Art and Technology
in 1979–80, she completed a degree in fine art at Stourbridge
College, near Birmingham, in 1983. Since 1983 Boyce has
exhibited in Britain and abroad, and lectured extensively. She
lives and works in London.

Education

1973 – 1979
Eastlea Comprehensive School
Canning Town East London

1979 – 1980
East Ham College of Art and Technology
Foundation Course Art & Design

1980 – 1983
Stourbridge College of Technology and Art
BA Degree Fine Art

Solo Exhibitions

1986
'Conversations'
Black Art Gallery, London
'Sonia Boyce', Air Gallery, London – catalogue

1988
'Recent Work', Whitechapel Art Gallery, London – catalogue

1991
'Something Else', Vanessa Devereux Gallery, London

1993
'Do You Want To Touch?', 181 Gallery, London

1995
'PEEP', Brighton Museum – catalogue

Group Exhibitions

1983
'Five Black Women', Africa Centre, London
'Black Woman Time Now', Battersea Arts Centre, London

1984
'Strip Language', Gimpel Fils, London – catalogue
'Into The Open', Mappin Art Gallery, Sheffield – catalogue
'Heroes And Heroines', Black Art Gallery, London

1985
'Room At The Top', Nicola Jacobs Gallery, London – catalogue
'Blackskins/Bluecoat', Bluecoat Gallery, Liverpool
'Celebration/Demonstration', St Matthews Meeting Place, London
'No More Little White Lies', Chapter Arts Centre, Cardiff
'Reflections', Riverside Studios, London
'The Thin Black Line', ICA, London – catalogue
'From Generation To Generation', Black Art Gallery, London

1986
'Some Of Us Are Brave – All Of Us Are Strong', Black Art
Gallery, London
'Unrecorded Truths', Elbow Room, London – catalogue
'From Two Worlds', Whitechapel Art Gallery, London – catalogue
'Caribbean Expressions In Britain', Leicestershire Museum and
Art Gallery, and tour – catalogue
'Basel Art Fair', (with Gimpel Fils), Switzerland
'State Of The Art', ICA, London and tour – book and tv series
'A Cabinet Of Drawings', Gimpel Fils, London

1987
'The Image Employed – The Use Of Narrative In Black Art',
Cornerhouse, Manchester – catalogue
'Critical Realism', Nottingham Castle Museum and Art Gallery,
and tour – catalogue
'Basel Art Fair', (with Gimpel Fils), Switzerland
'Royal Overseas League', London – catalogue

1988
'The Essential Black Art', Chisenhale Gallery, London and tour
– catalogue
'The Impossible Self', Winnipeg Art Gallery, Winnipeg and tour
– catalogue
'The Thatcher Years', Angela Flowers Gallery, London
'Fashioning Feminine Identities', University of Essex, Colchester
'Along The Lines Of Resistance', Cooper Art Gallery, Barnsley
and tour – catalogue

1989
'The Wedding', Mappin Art Gallery, Sheffield – catalogue
'The Other Story', Hayward Art Gallery, London and tour
– catalogue
'The Cuban Biennale', Wifredo Lam Cultural Centre, Havana

1990
'The British Art Show', McLellan Galleries, Glasgow and tour
– catalogue
'Distinguishing Marks', University of London – catalogue
'The Invisible City', Photographers Gallery, London – catalogue
'Black Markets', Cornerhouse, Manchester and tour

1991
'Delfina Open Studios', London
'Shocks To The System', South Bank Centre, London and tour
– catalogue
'Delfina Annual Summer Show', London – catalogue
'An English Summer' Palazzo della Crepadona, Belluna, Italy
'Photo Video', Photographers Gallery, London and tour

1992
'Delfina Annual Summer Show', London – catalogue
'White Noise', IKON Gallery, Birmingham – publication
'Northern Adventures', Camden Arts Centre and St Pancras
Station, London – publication
'Nosepaint Artist Club', London
'Innocence And Experience', Manchester City Art Galleries, and
tour – catalogue

1993
'New England Purpose Built: Long Distance Information' Real
Art Ways, Hartford, USA

1994
'Thinking Aloud', Small Mansions Art Centre, London
'Wish You Were Here', BANK, London and tour – catalogue
'Glass Vitrine', INIVA Launch, London

1995
'Free Stories', LA Galerie, Frankfurt
'Portable Fabric Shelters', London Printworks Trust, London –
catalogue
'Fetishism', Brighton Museum, Brighton and tour – catalogue
'Mirage', ICA, London – catalogue
'Photogenetic', Street Level, Glasgow and tour
'Cottage Industry', Beaconsfield, London – catalogue

1996
'Picturing Blackness in British Art', Tate Gallery, London
– publication
'Kiss This', Focalpoint Gallery, Southend

Selected Bibliography

1983
Moremi Charles, 'Beyond Labels', *City Limits*
Sarah Kent, 'Five Black Women Artists', *Time Out*

1984
Waldemar Januszczk, 'Into The Open', *The Guardian*

1986
David Lee, 'Sonia Boyce Air Gallery', *Arts Review*
Eddie Chambers and Tam Joseph, *The Arts Pack*

1987
Mary Rose Beaumont, 'Sonia Boyce Air Gallery', *Arts Review*
Michael Archer, 'Sonia Boyce Air Gallery', *Artforum*
Maud Sulter, 'Sonia Boyce Air Gallery', *Spare Rib*
Fiona Barber, 'Sonia Boyce Octagon Gallery', *Circa*
'Dossier: Five Black Women Artists', *Framing Feminism*, ed.
Rozsika Parker and Griselda Pollock
Lubaina Himid, 'We Will Be', *Looking On*, ed. Rosemary
Betterton

1988
Louisa Buck, 'Sonia Boyce Recent Work', *City Limits*
Elorine Grant, 'Sonia Boyce Recent Work', *Spare Rib*
Tony Warner, 'Framing Feminine Identity', *Arts Review*
Robert Clark, 'Barnsley's Line Of Most Resistance', *The Guardian*
'Sonia Boyce in Conversation with John Roberts', *Third Text*
Sutapa Biswas and Marlene Smith, 'Will The Art Critic Please
Step Forward', *Spare Rib*
Sonia Boyce, 'Talking In Tongues', *Storms Of The Heart*, ed.
Kwesi Owusu
Amanda Holiday, 'Employing The Image' (video)

1989
Rita Keegan, 'The Story So Far', *Spare Rib*
Lorraine Griffiths, 'Black Women In The Arts', *The Voice*
'40 Under 40 – The New Generation', *Art and Design magazine*

1990
Genevieve Fox, 'The Invisible City', *Art Monthly*
Gilane Tawadros, 'Beyond The Boundary: The Work Of Three
Black Women Artists', *Third Text*
John Roberts, *Postmodernism Politics and Art*
Whitney Chadwick, 'Women Art and Society'
Penny Dunford, *A Biographical Dictionary of Women Artists
in Britain and America Since 1850*
Kobena Mercer, 'The Burden of Representation' (tv), *Open
University*

1991
Charles Hall, 'Sonia Boyce' *Arts Review*
Interview between Elorine Grant and Sonia Boyce, 'Something
Else', *Spare Rib*

1992
'The Thin Black Line' (republished), *Urban Fox Press*
'The Critical Decade', *Ten-8*
Stuart Hall, 'Reconstruction Work' *The Critical Decade*, *Ten-8*
'The Art Show', *BBC Television*
Sonia Boyce and Manthia Diawara, 'The Art Of Identity: A
Conversation', *Transition 55*

1993
Tania Guha, 'Do You Want To Touch?', *Time Out*

1994

'Thinking Aloud', *Womens Art Magazine*
Sarah Kent, 'Wish You Were Here', *Time Out*
Liam Gillick, 'Wish You Were Here', *Art Monthly*
'Missionary Position II – Position Changing', 1985, *Tate Gallery Catalogue Entry*
'From Tarzan To Rambo', 1987, *Tate Gallery Catalogue Entry*

1995

James Hall, 'Object Lesson', *The Guardian*
Sarah Kent, 'Body Politic', *Time Out*
'Pick Of The Day', *The Independent*
Richard Cork, 'Mirage', *The Times*
Christian Haye, 'Just An Illusion', *Frieze*
Tommy Lott, 'King Kong Lives: Racist Discourse and the Negro-Ape Metaphor, *Next Of Kin: Looking At, The Great Apes catalogue*

1996

Kobena Mercer, 'Home From Home: Portraits From Places In Between', *Self Evident catalogue*
Sonia Boyce and Manthia Diawara, 'The Art Of Identity: A Conversation', *Black Cultural Studies A Reader* (reprint)

Photo Credits

p. 2, 181 Gallery, London
p. 6, 181 Gallery, London, private collection
p. 6, 181 Gallery, London
p. 6, 181 Gallery, London
p. 9, Anne Cardale, private collection
p. 9, Anne Cardale, collection: Tate Gallery
p. 10, Women's Art Library, collection: Cleveland Museum
p. 13, Anne Cardale, private collection
pp. 14 and 15, Peter Burton and Michael Pollard
p. 21, collection: Victoria and Albert Museum
pp. 24 & 25, David Catchpole
p. 28, Ka-che Kary Kwok, private collection
p. 32, Anne Cardale, private collection
pp. 34 and 35, Arts Council, collection: Arts Council of Great Britain
p. 37, Black Art Gallery, private collection
p. 38, Edward Woodman, private collection
p. 40, Arts Council, collection: Arts Council of Great Britain
p. 43, Royal Overseas League, private collection
pp. 44 and 45, Tate Gallery, collection: Tate Gallery
p. 54, Helen Juffs, courtesy: IKON Gallery
p. 55, Helen Juffs, courtesy: IKON Gallery
p. 65, Chris Lienhard, collection: British Council
p. 67, Beaconsfield
p. 76, private collection
p. 78, South Bank Centre
p. 79, London Printworks Trust
p. 81, London Printworks Trust
p. 82, Chris Lienhard
p. 85, Chris Lienhard, private collection
pp. 88, 89, 90 and 91, private collection

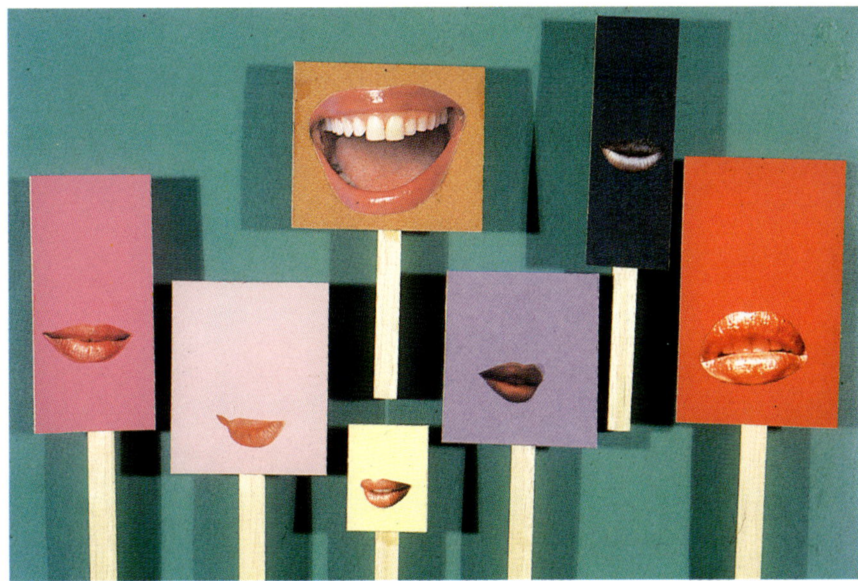

Preaching To The Converted 1995
maquette for placards

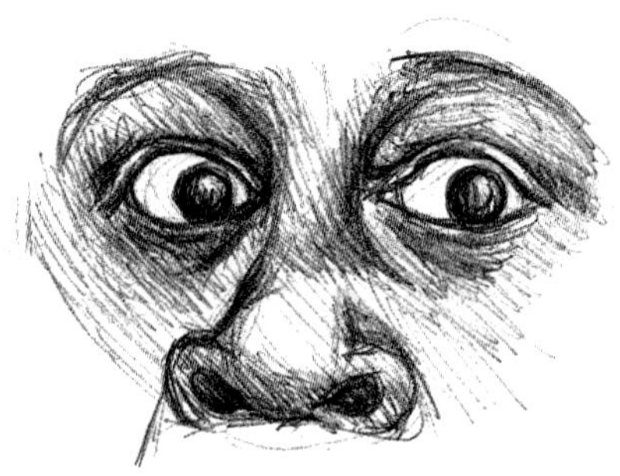

sketchbook drawing of actor Manton Moreland
from a film still of *The Jade Mask* 1987